MAKE YOUR OWN LUCK

MAKE YOUR OWN LUCK

A DIY ATTITUDE TO GRAPHIC DESIGN & ILLUSTRATION

Kate Moross
Foreword by **Neville Brody**

PRESTEL

Munich ⚡ **London** ⚡ New York

FOREWORD

Kate Moross is nuts. Brilliant, creative, fun and unique. And obsessed. You have to be. To not only survive but prosper in this industry requires all the driven craziness you can muster.

From a beginning in flyers, fanzines and fanciful failures, Kate has forged her own path. Growing up as part of the lively independent music scene in London, she has grabbed the chance to develop and flourish within a supportive community packed with opportunities and challenges. Her ceaseless energy and hunger for new ideas and new inventions has led her to be constantly experimenting, always pushing boundaries. Energetically embracing the possibility of failure is a far greater venture than playing safe.

We share a lot, Kate and I. North Londoners, we both went to art school in South London, and survived, and then pursued careers driven by our interests in radical and often politicized underground music. On leaving the London College of Printing, I had the luxury of being connected to the burgeoning UK music scene. Like Kate, I produced fanzines and music posters at college, and the nascent independent record industry consequently allowed me to both earn a meagre living and drive my ideas at the same time. I lived in a squat, and again like her was obsessed, working virtually 24-hour days, seven days a week. I felt that if you weren't obsessed by developing what you were doing, you should be pursuing something else.

I first met Kate in 2005 at the London College of Communication as part of a onedotzero workshop called TypoMove. We have had intermittent connections since then, largely through Kate kindly dropping off the odd piece of misdelivered post to my studio in Angel — Kate's mum is our neighbour here! In 2013 we met up at Typo Berlin and found out just how much we have in common. Kate had presented a lecture, and I was amazed at the quality of and creative thinking behind the work and at just how sure and confident Kate was.

The other thing that surprised me was the breadth of work. Kate is unafraid to jump between media and platforms, living out the premise that we are all becoming multi-disciplinarians; that the modern designer is hybrid and operating across any platform, be it illustration, typography, print, video, installation, programming, web, app, sound, fashion, writing or food! Kate's roster of clients is testimony to her unlimited scope, quality of thinking and professionalism — be it Diesel, Adidas, Eastpak or Retro Super Future; *Vice, Vogue* or the *New York Times*; Jessie Ware, Pictureplane, Simian Mobile Disco or Apes and Androids.

In this book, Kate has pulled together invaluable advice from that experience to help young creatives who want to start out on this journey, peppered with plentiful examples of her work. It isn't easy, this business of ours, and a creative designer is by nature driven and rarely satisfied, but it is one of the most rewarding professions you can possibly think of jumping into. Good luck.

Neville Brody
London, 2014

When I first started out as a graphic designer and illustrator, I worked mainly for the growing circle of friends and contacts I made as I explored London as a young and enthusiastic music fan. I followed a simple DIY ethos inspired by the riot grrrl and punk music culture that I had been absorbing since my teenage years through pirated music, gigs, zines and, more importantly, the Internet. Whether it was creating my first zine using a photocopier or selling promo posters I'd made at a gig, this do it / make it / design it yourself attitude was something I picked up from the different things I was into. But as much as I wished I had been at those early Bikini Kill concerts, the reality was that I grew up in England listening to (and coming up with dance routines for) the Spice Girls' 'Say You'll Be There'.

While it might seem embarrassing to admit that I used to spend my time dancing around to the Spice Girls in homemade polystyrene platform trainers, the merchandized product of Girl Power was hugely influential on me, and music undoubtedly became one of the most important things in my life. Surrounded by a family of music lovers, I soon discovered my older brother's diverse CD collection and through it the music of Jamiroquai, Cake, The Bangles, Carly Simon, Stevie Wonder, Simon and Garfunkel, Toni Braxton and Motown, which all featured in the soundtrack of my childhood.

Another important part of my upbringing was the time I spent each year at a Jewish summer camp in the English countryside. From the tender age of seven, for two weeks of the summer holidays, I was thrust into a crowd of screaming children, art classes and innumerable activities ranging from outdoor games to bubble writing on posters, guitar playing and trying not to wake the grown-ups. More than anything else, the experience was a social one. Initially I was new to the environment and the crowd, but each year I'd learn more, and eventually I was one of the big girls teaching and leading activity groups. Summer camp instilled in me a fierce independence and an easy confidence around people, whether they were familiar or strangers.

By the age of 17 I'd turned my self-confidence into activity: I was the designer of the school magazine and was decorating the sets for school plays, illustrating the cover of the yearbook and spending every second of my spare time teaching myself new software on the art department's computer. If there was a creative job to be done, I was the first one to volunteer.

I brought this attitude, as well as my love of music, to Camberwell College of Arts in 2006, where I studied graphic design. I became practically nocturnal, relishing the chance to embed myself in the London music scene and taking photographs of bands at gigs with my Canon 350D. I also bought my first Wacom tablet and started drawing and posting my creations online. As well as taking people's pictures at clubs I drew vector portraits, posting them on people's MySpace profiles, and offered my services as a MySpace coder for bands and club nights. I designed a few profile skins and I don't think I took any payment — I was just happy to have something to do. Everyone, it seemed, had a moniker and needed a logo, so with a student copy of Adobe Illustrator I became an unstoppable logo-maker, creating avatars for practically everyone I met.

As well as HTML, which I learned through creating custom MySpace skins, I taught myself Dreamweaver so I could start to work as a web designer. I built early websites for the Young Turks record label, The Maccabees and Lightspeed Champion, to name just a few. This is how I started doing flyers — I was using a basic requirement such as a website or logo to promote myself as a designer. It worked.

Essentially I had started freelancing before I really knew what it meant to be a designer. I was hungry to establish myself as someone who could bring design to different music-related areas, so I took on whatever I could. And because I didn't know much, I learned a lot fast. That's why, primarily, this book exists — to pass on some of those lessons and help people understand that my success hasn't just happened overnight. I didn't emerge into the world with a fully formed style or approach. Rather I've worked hard for years, not just at learning the tools of my trade and experimenting with different visual ideas and materials, but at being an asset to my peers, who together formed a busy community of like-minded, driven young people who wanted to make something of themselves and of their endeavours. Of course, to succeed you need some good fortune as well as good skills, but in my experience, if you work hard and do whatever you can for whoever you can, well, you might just make your own luck.

Me at Studio Moross, 2013

Speaking from my own personal experience at Camberwell College of Arts, art school is what you make of it. A first-class degree is nothing without real-life experience, so it is your job to create work, initiate projects and find your way through the syllabus. This is not a criticism: I believe that this approach can teach you very valuable skills, and the lecturers are always present to critique your work and guide you. This way of learning can be difficult, though, as you will have to maintain enthusiasm and motivation across short- and long-term projects, some of which you might not enjoy. Learning to find your own way through a project is a challenge, but also a skill that will be very useful when you have graduated.

My advice is to complete your coursework as best you can, and if you can add extra outcomes to a project, do it, even if it is not required. For example, if you are asked to design a poster, do a series; if the brief is to develop a brand identity, sketch out a website and a set of stationery to complement your work. Document your working process and help the tutors understand the choices you make, as this will help them assess your work. Attend lectures and seminars — dodging classes won't get you anywhere. Crits are VERY important: learning how to communicate your work is key. If you aren't naturally talented at giving presentations, these sessions will be good practice for you to develop this crucial skill. It is also a great idea to challenge, question and make suggestions to your peers (constructively, of course). This will demonstrate to your tutor your critical thinking and design understanding — and who knows, you might even end up helping a friend with something they have been struggling with.

hello you

THE SUBJECTIVE TUTOR

Art teachers have strong opinions. They may HATE your work; they may not get it. Sometimes they will be right, and sometimes they are wrong. Trust your instincts. Yes, you are being graded and you want to do well, but believe in your creative direction. If you disagree strongly with your tutor, swallow a bad grade and see your work through. The grade is evaluated by looking at the supporting work, concept, development of ideas and documentation. As long as you do these, regardless of whether your work is to your teacher's taste, you should be marked fairly and objectively. If you feel that the work has not been marked fairly, you can appeal to your head of year for a second opinion.

GET AHEAD

University is great fun and hugely educational, but it's not the be all and end all. Having a Bachelor of Arts degree doesn't make you employable; experience is just as important. Personally, when I read a job application I don't look at the CV until after I have looked at (and liked) the portfolio. The three most important things to me are the body of work, communication skills and personality. If I'm impressed by all of these I'll hire you on the spot, regardless of any grades and degrees. Therefore you should use university, its facilities and the awesome new community you have discovered there to generate work. Though warehouse parties, guest list events and student exhibitions are tempting, set some free time aside for working on your own projects. Some university courses only need you to be in the studio one day a week; others can require that you attend for 40 hours a week, with strict registration. But no matter what course you are on, you should be making your own work, whether it be in response to personal briefs you have set yourself, competition briefs, freelance projects or interning. If you're worried about fitting it all in, discuss any concerns with your tutors; maybe they will allow for a live project to be included in your course structure or end of term marks. Expanding your portfolio is essential. If you start freelancing now, the transition to professional life after finishing your degree will be much easier.

Don't label university projects as such on your website; there is no need to point these out to whoever is viewing your portfolio. Your work should all blend together.

BOYS

THE 10,000-HOUR RULE

Design is as practical a subject as any other academic area, and you must put in many hours of practice in order to do it well. The theory of the 10,000-hour rule says that anyone who spends this much time learning something will become an expert in it, or beyond. The more time you spend working in your software, the better you will be at using it. Give me any problem in Illustrator and I can solve it, because I have been using the software since before it was bundled with Creative Suite in 2003. Using it every day for over 10 years has been worthwhile!

The most important thing you can do during your time at university is learn how to use the tools at your disposal. These are imperative for professional practice. Even if you don't want to create digital work, software is an essential tool. You have to recognize that at some point or another your work will pass through a computer, whether it is photographing large-format paintings, scanning technical drawings, archiving your work for your website or generating digital work. The computer is essential: it's as simple as that. Even if you aim to be a fine artist, you will need to earn money somehow in the interim and computer / software skills will come in handy.

Art school isn't meant to be easy. Some days you will feel like you are in a therapy session, and on other days you will feel totally lost, but whatever happens, work hard and listen harder. Find a tutor who understands you, who you can go to for honest advice. If your teachers don't like your work, don't shy away and give up; prove them wrong. Fulfil all your examination requirements. Even if they don't like your topic, style or theme, if you hand in the work that is required, you can still do well.

OR DON'T GO TO UNIVERSITY?

University is more expensive than ever, so you might wonder whether the ensuing debt will be worth it. My opinion is that it's not essential. If you have a full- or part-time day job, build your creative work experience around it. Contribute your creative skills to your company and help with the creative aspects of the job. Use your free time to start doing small live projects: help out a family friend with a website, take pictures at a wedding, draw portraits. Whatever you want to start doing, just do it. You have three years to catch up with those university students, so use your time sensibly. Take some evening classes, or teach yourself the software you need using online tutorials. There are plenty of student briefs openly available on which you can test your skills. Use forums to post your outcomes, discuss and receive feedback on your work and approach practising professionals for advice on your portfolio. Document your work and build up your portfolio; get to know the trade you want to get into; save up and buy the equipment you need to start work. You can seek freelance work, too; work experience is the most important element when learning to be a designer. There are plenty of self-taught practitioners out there, and a degree doesn't make a designer. Good luck, and work your arse off.

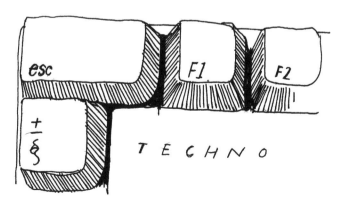

My mother always told me that if I wanted to be an artist, I had to draw all the time — that practice is what makes you excel. She said I must always carry a sketchbook on me, so I got into the habit of doing this. Although I am an illustrator, I rarely do anything observational or figurative; my work is nearly all type-based.

Hand-drawing letterforms is something I have always done. As a young child I used to copy book covers and make my own versions of popular children's books. I used to draw band logos meticulously over and over again in my sketchbooks at school. I was never great at drawing objects or people, but words and letters felt like a natural subject for me.

The art of lettering is ancient and I am really thankful for the resurgence in hand-lettering in recent years. It has been and always will be a core element in design and our visual landscape. No matter how digital our lives become, hand-rendered type reminds us of our humanity.

Looking back on these doodles makes me appreciate the way I used to draw and think. Years of briefs and client work have stifled this freedom in me; rarely now can I just sit down in front of a blank page and create work. These days, I feel as though I need someone looking over my shoulder and directing me. Drawing just for the sake of it is something I aim to get back into — I am just waiting for some free time!

I implore you, if you enjoy it, never stop drawing, especially for yourself. The skills that drawing hones will stand you in good stead.

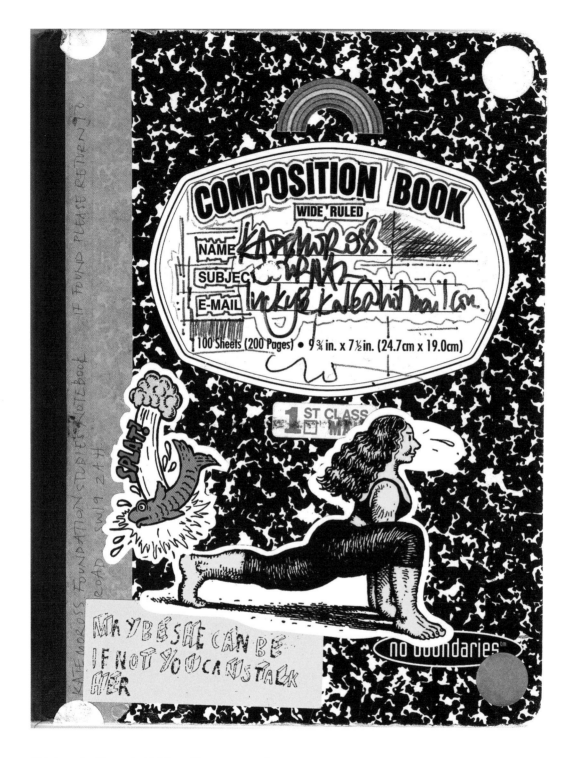

This is my first journal which I used to carry around
and draw in as a teenager; I'd stick the work of artists
I loved (like Robert Crumb and Dr Seuss) on the front
to constantly motivate me

BRAIN FOR SALE

IN GWO

UNWANTED BIRTHDAY PRESENT

£ 10 ONO   +   POSTAGE + PACKAGING.

(CAN BE COLLECTED) MAY LEAK IN YOUR CAR?

CALL: 0781 115 2513 ASK FOR KATE

DRAW TOGETHER FANZINE

I had a nice little collection of zines back in 2006, when I started listening to riot grrrl music, so I thought it was about time I made my own. I had managed to get my hands on a redundant photocopier that my dad's office was throwing out. I collected it in a minicab and had it installed in my bedroom. I'm pretty sure all the electrical safety certificates had expired!

I made my very first zine, entitled *Draw Together*, over the summer of 2006. I only made around 30 copies and gave them out to various people. The first ten came with a badge. Yes, I also have a badge machine — I was living the DIY dream! I'd bought it to start a badge-making company, but that venture didn't get beyond a website.

SICK OF NATURE FLYERS →

I don't think I'll ever stop enjoying illustrating lots of copy. So when a brief like this one comes along, where the client just wants me to draw words I fancy anyway, I oblige.

Although the first Sick of Nature monthly flyers were created by the illustrator Tobias Jones, he was busy one month, so passed the task over to me. For each gig I was to draw up a flyer and a poster. I had really got into the hand-drawn groove by then, and I wanted to push it even further, so every month I came up with original fonts for each member of the line-up. These posters were seminal in establishing me as an illustrator, since they ended up everywhere, and even after the night stopped running, people remembered the flyers. They were plastered around East London in all of their CMYK glory.

I never really plan a drawing. I just sit down in front of a blank page and go for it. I have never been precious about my drawings; I just think of them as sketches and scraps of paper. That way they don't intimidate me, and I can't mess them up. I make mistakes all the time, but try to work them back into the picture somehow. That's a great skill to learn as an illustrator: how to hide your mistakes and make them into happy accidents. I sometimes work in pencil, but I use a light box to trace the pen version onto a clean sheet of paper. That way, I still have my original sketch to trace from, just in case I need to start again. The Sick of Nature drawings are full of mistakes; see how many you can spot!

IF YOU COULD

If You Could was the brainchild of students Alex Bec and Will Hudson, who would go on to found the It's Nice That blog and creative agency. The project saw them approach dozens of image-makers, both up-and-coming and well-established, to ask them to respond to this simple brief: if you could do anything tomorrow, what would it be?

This print was part of a series that was screenprinted to order every month. The number of prints sold within the month determined the edition. I didn't technically finish my design — I left a large section undrawn (check out the top of the illustration) — but I liked it like that, so I just left it.

Opposite: Atlantic Records nominees at the 2013 Grammy Awards

Sometimes you shouldn't finish your work in the way you'd originally envisaged. Leaving it slightly unfinished can make it look more unexpected. Trust your instincts.

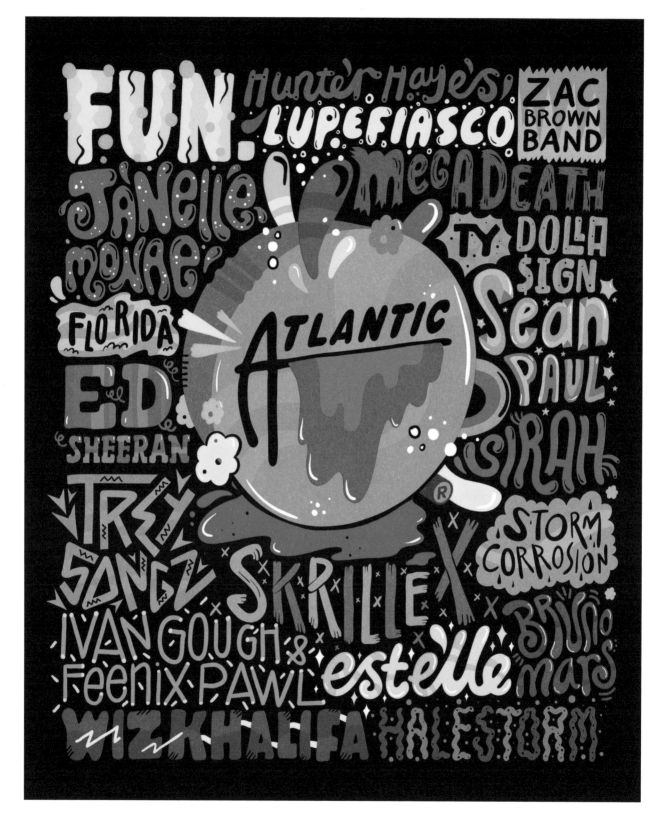

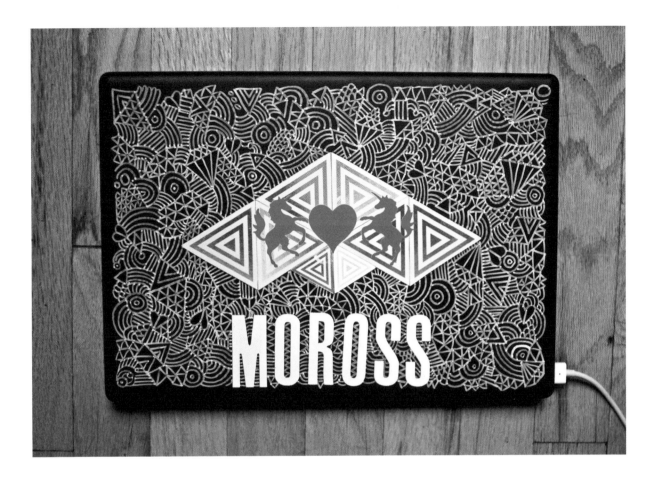

MACBOOK DOODLE

When my cracked MacBook Pro stopped working completely in 2006
(I fell asleep on it, oops), I purchased a cheaper MacBook to replace it. Big
mistake. It definitely couldn't handle the way I work, using lots of programs
at the same time and working with high-res files. I had to buy ANOTHER
machine to work on, and this MacBook came on tour with me when I briefly
joined the band Heartsrevolution as their VJ (see page 105). Seeing as it
was going to be on stage with us, it couldn't be plain and boring, so a little
bit of decoration was in order.

DIESEL:U:MUSIC RADIO MURAL

For Diesel:U:Music Radio's new studios on London's Kingsland Road, I decorated a party wall just like a party wall should be decorated — with confetti and everything. No grids or rules, just lots of practice and a steady hand!

I wouldn't worry too much about style. Style is temporary anyway, and it's more important to have good ideas and a honed craft. Even though you will naturally illustrate in a certain way (it's hard to change how you draw), it is all too easy to imitate styles you've seen before. This is why it's important to experiment with different techniques and methods. You may find you enjoy doing type, pattern, portraits, landscapes, line drawing or digital work. Just keep illustrating — over time your own style will emerge.

I'm not a figurative illustrator. I love working with type and abstract shapes, so this way of working has become my style, I suppose. I often get jobs that push my boundaries and challenge my natural style — I may need to draw people, spaces or objects, for example — but I will always think of a way to answer a particular brief in my own way, doing what I enjoy.

Style is dangerous: it can go in and out of fashion or date quickly. The most important thing is that your images have a quirk over and above aesthetics. This might be humour, naivety or wit; maybe they have layered meaning, or stories hidden in the detail; or perhaps they are super simple but execute the concept perfectly. It is these things that make an illustration more than just a picture. As veteran graphic designer and illustrator Bob Gill says, 'Have an opinion.' People will pay you for it.

TROUBLE CONCERTS IN ASSOCIATION WITH DROWNED IN SOUND & YOUNG TURKS PRESENTS...

BY KATE MOROSS

www.trouble-events.com

SATURDAY AUG 26TH

ANIMAL COLLECTIVE LIVE IN CONCERT AT A WAREHOUSE IN EAST LONDON CABLE ST STUDIOS UNIT 7, CABLE STREET 566 E1 0AH

TICKETS £8 IN ADVANCE TICKETWEB.CO.UK

ANIMAL COLLECTIVE POSTER

When local promoter Blaise Bellville asked me to draw an Animal Collective poster for an upcoming gig in 2006, I did it for free because I liked the band and wanted to go to the show. I sold A3 copies on the night to make my money back.

What I ended up with is now one of my earliest recognizable poster designs. The aesthetic blended well with the sound and ethos of the band. If you have one of these posters (I probably even wrote your initials on it and held onto it for you while you watched the show), please look after it, as I only printed and sold 25 of them — I didn't even keep one for myself!

These days, I rarely have the chance to get down to gigs to sell posters, but back then I was dedicated. I printed them for £1 each and sold them for £3. I didn't get paid to design the poster, but I made £50 selling them due to my DIY determination.

GAMBLE SKATEBOARDS

French skateboard company Gamble had the best idea I'd ever heard of for a skateboard design: each of its decks was covered in the same silver coating as a scratch card. You have to ride the board to reveal the artwork underneath over time through wear and tear. The idea was so great I just had to have my art under there!

FACT Magazine cover, 2007

FACT ILLUSTRATION

In October 2006 *FACT* asked me to illustrate its top musical projects
of the year for a page in its magazine. For this commission, the guys
wanted me to work along the lines of all the different 'logos' I had created
on the Sick of Nature flyers (see pages 23–25). This became a recurring
theme when fielding commissions — I was repeatedly asked to create
similar work.

 As an illustrator, being asked to replicate the same style is common. Sometimes you fight it, and sometimes you do what you are asked. The best thing is to compromise: do what the client wants, but don't spread your style too thin. Use it as an opportunity to make small changes and then it will grow project by project.

ALL AGES CONCERTS

Once I had successfully designed a couple of flyers for bands and promoters, the door opened to a whole gamut of extra illustrations. All Ages asked for a logo and several flyers, a perfect opportunity for me to develop my own hand while lending my aesthetic to an event, making it recognizable.

Creating work is just as much about lending your hand to a brand as it is about making something for yourself.

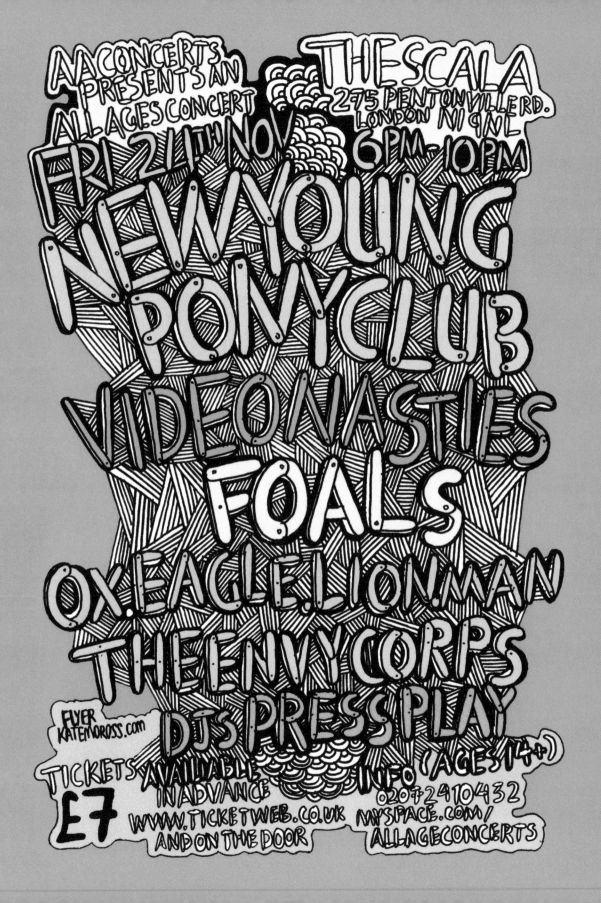

WHAT'S WRONG WITH INSPIRATION?

What inspires me? Please don't ask …

For some reason, the question 'What inspires you?' really annoys me.
I get asked it a lot and I don't really know why it irks me so much. Maybe
it's because I rarely feel 'inspired' in the corny way that inspiration is
depicted in movies and stories. Or maybe it's because it seems like such
a lazy question.

Draft cover for the
New York Times Magazine
'Inspiration Issue', 2013

The truth is, I don't go to galleries and exhibitions or look at art books and magazines for inspiration. I do these things because I find them interesting, but generally feel that what I see and soak up in this way has very little correlation to my work. In fact, I find some image sources, such as Tumblr and Pinterest, to be the very antithesis of inspiring — I find myself conscious of the fact that I'm looking at what has already been done, rather than moving forward and creating something new. Filling my head with other people's ideas and styles stunts my own by making less room for original thought.

At my studio we are making a conscious decision to move away from these things — to use materials as inspiration rather than referencing existing imagery. We want to have good ideas that aren't about style or what's popular right now, but finding a concept that fits the brief, or a material that can be used to illustrate it.

My best suggestion for finding the dreaded 'inspiration' is to look a little closer to home. Think about what interests you. Perhaps it's food, sport, literature or physics — ideas can come from all of these things. Pull ideas from areas that are missing visuals, rather than mimicking ones that already exist. Explore these wider topics and you will discover things that you can incorporate into your work which are far more interesting than anything you find online. Trends and styles come in and out of fashion quickly, but collections, archives and detailed studies of single topics will always be interesting and will be personal to you and the development of your work.

Everyone collects something or other, so instead of collecting other people's styles, try to find an area to research and document for yourself. For me, it's the packaging of sweets and candy. Aside from having a very sweet tooth, I adore sweet packaging — I think it is some of the finest design around. The typography is usually so direct and complete, illustrating what is inside the wrapper perfectly. Every single sweet wrapper also evokes a strong and everlasting nostalgia in anyone who used to enjoy them as a child. The simple colour palettes and often hand-rendered typography definitely influenced me when I was a child, and to this day I continue to pay homage to bubblegum type in my own work.

Mmm … maybe I've just answered that question I hate so much!

NETWORKING and SELF PROMOTION

In the early stages of my career, everywhere I went was a networking opportunity. I was discovering London and meeting new people every week. Expanding my social circle wasn't the result of a carefully calculated campaign on my part; it's just what happens in a big city when you have a big mouth!

I was lucky to have started my career at the dawn of social media. MySpace was just hitting the UK and it was the first platform I found on which to share my work with my peers. Because I had bought my own domain name, katemoross.com, my page stood out and people took notice. Nobody cared how old I was or if I was still at school; they saw my website and hired me.

Of course, these days, standing out from everyone else is much harder and success is going to come from a combination of hard work and skill at getting your name and work out there. From my own experience, here are a few practical tips that you can follow.

Get a website. No excuses.
There is no excuse not to have a website these days. Every freelancer, whatever their trade, should have a website where people can view a selection of their works. There are many resources you can use that are either free or of minimal cost, such as Indexhibit, Cargo Collective, Squarespace, Tumblr, Behance, WordPress and Blogger.

Invest a small amount of money in buying a suitable domain name. If you want to come across as a pro, then the old lucky8_kate@hotmail.com email address isn't so impressive. It's far better to use the new domain you purchased to host your emails so you can upgrade your contact details accordingly. All this attention to detail will elevate you above someone who hasn't made a similar effort.

A simple gallery template is the perfect foundation for your website. First impressions are crucial, so choose strong pieces which you feel best represent your approach.

Scan your drawings and photograph your larger-format work and books. Make your images big, smart and shiny. Keep the descriptions of work on your site concise and double-check the spelling. If you find writing about your work difficult, ask someone to check through it for you, or just keep it to one sentence. Always credit your collaborators.

Self-Promote

Now that you have a website and a corresponding email address, you can make business cards. Keep some in your pocket and remember to use them. Every new connection you make is important. I can trace every early job back to a social encounter. Back in 2007, people weren't Googling 'graphic designer London' and finding my site; rather, I was pointing people I met in the real world to it. Don't be afraid to tell people what you do. Be confident in yourself. Word will spread, and hey! you have a website, so they can look you up or pass you on. People love to share contacts and help their friends, so make it easy for them.

Once you get your first few jobs, it goes without saying that you should do them to the best of your ability. Make sure they are AMAZING. Astound your client, over-deliver — it is, quite simply, good business. The new network you are building relies on these early clients to spread the good word about your work. Think about it like a family tree: the early jobs are your children, and it is through them that a legacy will be built. My first few projects as a freelancer were the most crucial, and I approached each one in the same way: I worked incredibly hard at fulfilling the brief and I did the job well. As a result, each client asked me to do more work. I had lots of repeat business and these first clients recommended me to others as well, and the work that I was generating filled up my portfolio. That meant I was booked to do more, similar work, and so the hand-drawn lettering style proliferated.

A word of warning here: in these early stages, only publish work to your website if you are keen to do more of the same. If a particular project represents ideas or styles you aren't keen on, don't showcase it, or you run the risk of being approached to create similar work. This isn't to say that you shouldn't take on the job — I have done many jobs that have never appeared on my site. It's not that I'm ashamed of the work or that I think it's bad; it just doesn't represent a direction that I want to explore further.

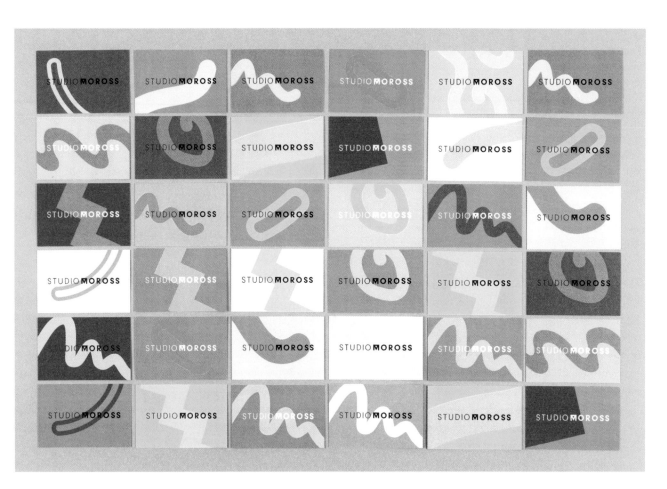

Studio Moross business cards, 2013

YOUNG TURKS FLYERS

People are your greatest resource. Be nice, show up, pull through and keep your promises. If I hadn't done that, there wouldn't be a book's worth of stuff for you to read.

I first met Caius Pawson in the queue for White Heat, a monthly music night I used to be a regular at (see page 47). Caius spoke of world domination and success in the music industry, club nights and record labels. I listened and chirped up that I could design websites. As a result, I built him the original website for the record label he founded, Young Turks, and made some flyers for him in February 2006. It went well and we kept in touch. From there things took off and his label became respected internationally.

Since that very first chance meeting outside a nightclub, Caius has introduced me to countless people that I have ended up working with. Although I can't prove it, I suspect he tells people nice things about me, which leads them to consider getting in touch and hiring me. So thanks Pawson, I owe you one!

Young Turks also ran a competition to design their logo. I think I was the only entrant, so I was picked for the task. The resulting logo has been printed on records by the likes of SBTRKT and The xx, and has adorned many a T-shirt too. If I've come up to you and said 'nice shirt' while you were wearing it, I didn't mean to sound obnoxious, it's just my way of saying hello!

FRIDAY 31ST · MARCH 2006

TROUBLED MINDS

9 + 5 PM AM

AT 333 OLD ST

TOP FLOOR HOSTED BY:
YOUNG TURKS
WITH
Rid'em & Booze
Fisherprice
Soundsystem

BASEMENT:
HOSTED BY:
THE HORRORS
VINCENT WITH LUDES
VINCENT
& THE
VILLAINS Les
INCOMPETENTS
X EROX TEENS

MAINROOM:
LETHAL BIZZLE
TEAM WITH
MEGA MIX Matthew
Wowow!
Pyrahh girls
Blaise Bellville

£10 ENTRANCE
£8 CONCESSIONS

tickets available at
WWW.TROUBLED-MINDS.COM
FLYER www.katemoss.com

FRIDAY 26TH · MAY 2006

TROUBLED MINDS

FLYER www.katemoss.com

9 + 5 PM AM

AT 333 OLD ST

UPSTAIRS
YOUNG TURKS
LILY ALLEN DJ SET
ADVENTURE PLAYGROUND LIVE
TEENS OF THAILAND
EL PLATE

BASEMENT HOSTED BY
THE HORRORS DJ SETS

THE NOISETTES
ROLAND SHANKS
JACK PEÑATE
& BAND
OPERA HOUSE

MAINROOM
JAMMER LIVE!
WITH MC KNUCKLES & EARS
PYRAHH GIRLS
TEAM MEGA MIX
MATTHEW STONE
! WOWOW!

£10 ENTRANCE
£8 CONCESSIONS

tickets available at WWW.TROUBLED-MINDS.COM
FAST TRACK QUEUE FOR ALL TICKET HOLDERS

FRIDAY 30TH · JUNE 2006

TROUBLED MINDS

FLYER www.katemoss.com

9 + 5 PM AM

AT 333 OLD ST

UPSTAIRS
YOUNG TURKS
TEENS OF THAILAND
THE PEÑATE BROTHERS
ADVENTURE
PLAYGROUND
LIVE

BASEMENT
HOSTED BY
THE HORRORS

ABSENTEE
METRONOMY
APARTMENT
CAJUN DANCE PARTY
JAKOBINARINA

MAINROOM
RADIOCLIT
UK APACHE LIVE!
MATTHEW STONE
!WOWOW!
TEAM MEGA MIX
PYRAHH GIRLS
BLAISE BELLVILLE

£10 ENTRANCE
£8 CONCESSIONS

tickets available at WWW.TROUBLED-MINDS.COM
FAST TRACK QUEUE FOR ALL TICKET HOLDERS

FRIDAY 29TH · SEPTEMBER 06

TROUBLED MINDS

9 + 5 PM AM

AT 333 OLD ST

UPSTAIRS
DJ LUCK
& MC NEAT
ADVENTURE
PLAYGROUND (LIVE)
Matthew !Wowow!
Real Gold

BASEMENT
Eighties Matchbox
B-Line Disaster (DJ set)
Neils Children
Metro Riots
Baxter Dury
586
Faris Rottor (DJ set)

MAINROOM
HOSTED BY
EXTRA SPECIAL
FEATURING

Mickey Finn
(OLD SKOOL CLASSICS SET)
Ragga Twins
(LIVE)
El Plate & Nasty Mcquaid
Plus Special guests

LOGO & FLYER katemoss.com

ALL TICKETS ON THE DOOR
£5 BEFORE 11PM £10 AFTER

TROUBLED MINDS

I drew the first of these flyers with a mouse but progressed to a tablet once I realized how bad the type looked on the green version. Though some clubs had a new designer every month, I was kept on to do the series, which I always enjoyed. I found it satisfying to slightly adapt and polish the original rather messy design concept over subsequent flyer designs. It was a great way to (not quite) perfect a piece of work.

I attended most of the events that I drew flyers for, and a lot of the time I got more work at the gigs. People got to know me as a person that did flyers, and it grew from there.

It doesn't hurt to be persistent, as long as you are polite.

WHITE HEAT →

I used to go out nearly every night of the week. Every Tuesday I was welcomed into White Heat, a club night where I made new friends and discovered emerging music, and for which I cut my hair every which way. I MAY have mentioned a few (hundred) times to the night's promoter, Matty Hall, that I would like to get my hands on the artwork for the club, and so when he finally relented and asked me to do a flyer, I asked the night's regular flyer designer Ferry Gouw (Mad Decent, Major Lazer, Space Dimension Controller) to collaborate with me. Together we constructed an elaborate world of isometric structures and perspectives fused with Ferry's twisted comic style. This was harder than it looks. Lots of grids and composites, a LOT of shading and colouring and many hours of work were required to render our fantasy world.

MYSTERY JETS AND SYD BARRETT MEMORIAL

When I met Milo Cordell he was managing the band Mystery Jets. He called me up to see if I'd work on ads and a fanzine for a Syd Barrett (of Pink Floyd fame) memorial show. I took it on and curated the work in the zine, which featured contributions by the acts playing at the show. We printed 250 and they were free to everyone who attended. Seeing my work in print was really rewarding but the best bit was that it was this project that opened my mind to the psychedelic posters of the 1960s and '70s. I spent hours sifting through poster after poster, hoping to lend this style to the zine. Little did I know that these influences would continue to filter through my work for years to come.

MYSTERY JETS ACOUSTIC TOUR

Work went well with Mystery Jets after the Syd Barrett memorial project and I went on to design the posters and merchandise for the band's acoustic UK tour. This job taught me some serious lessons. Creating the artwork was relatively straightforward but putting it into production wasn't. I decided to go with a hand-drawn aesthetic and applied this to a poster and a tour ad. It was after these were approved that I was asked to reproduce the tour ad in no less than ten different formats. Now imagine me hand-drawing a new version for each individual publication's ad space, all of which had their own specific formats, some of them just a few centimetres wide. Lesson learned.

If you can only achieve the results you want with a really backwards method, start there and then learn how to do it better. This particular story highlights the fact that before going ahead with creating a piece of work, it's best to find out exactly how it will be reproduced, so you can take the appropriate measures when creating your design / response to the brief.

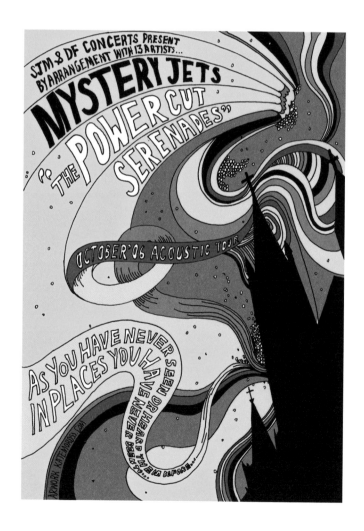

TOY PIRATE FANZINE

Toy Pirate is an A6 fanzine put together by Kev Bassett of long-lost band Lost Penguin. Kev emailed me out of the blue to tell me about the theme for an upcoming issue, which was simply 'BIG'.

It was around this time that I got in touch with the performance artist Scottee through Flickr and arranged to meet up. I mentioned *Toy Pirate* and asked if I could draw a picture of him for the 'BIG issue'. He of course obliged, and this was the result.

Social networks are as important to your work as they are to your social life. They can be a great way to connect with collaborators and clients.

Nightclubs can be great places to get work. Networking doesn't only happen at art openings and private views. ANYWHERE you can find like-minded people is an opportunity to find work. Some of my earliest commissions were secured while queuing for clubs or waiting at the bar for a cold glass of water.

IPOD BATTLE POSTER

In early 2007 I got a call from a girl with a cute French accent named Lolo, and we hit it off immediately. She was calling about an event called iPod Battle, which had been massively successful in France, and now it was time to bring it to London. The promoters needed 1,000 newsprint posters to be printed and folded up as flyers and asked me to design them.

This was the first time I had worked with such intricate isometric grids over a large area. My dedication to getting it right helped me to develop a new technique in Illustrator which transformed everything — I still use it today. On the back of the poster was a large yellow isometric grid in which you could create your own compositions.

After the event, Lolo sent me a photo that someone from an ad agency had emailed her — they had spelled out 'Nice Poster' by filling in my little triangles to create each letter. We did this entire project without ever meeting in real life. Perhaps unsurprisingly, we eventually met in a nightclub. Like Caius, Lolo has progressed in her career and, to some extent, taken me with along with her, commissioning me for further projects in 2009.

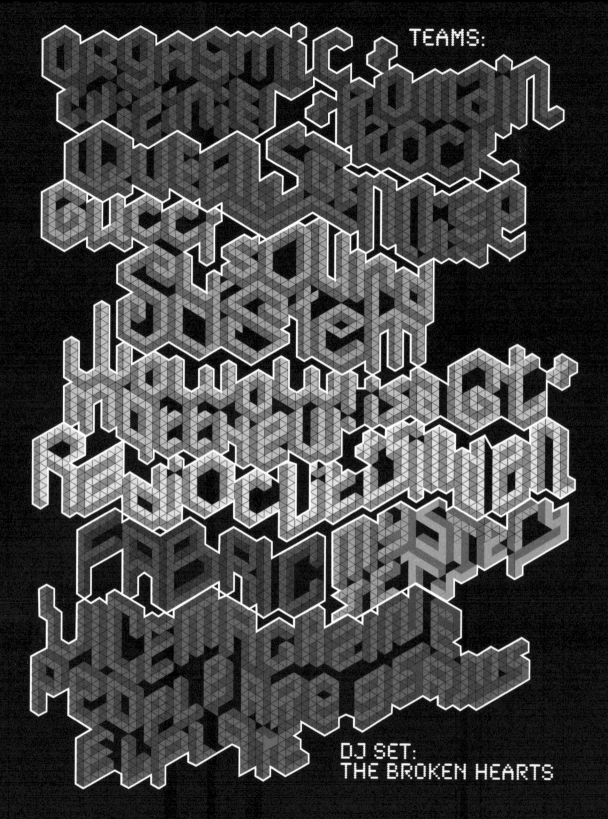

TEAMS:

ORGASMIC & ROMAIN

DJ SET:
THE BROKEN HEARTS

BETHNAL GREEN
WORKING MEN'S CLUB
42 POLLARD ROW
LONDON E2 6NB

MORE INFO ON:
WWW.MYSPACE.COM/OFFICIALUKIPODBATTLE
FLYER BY KATEMOROSS.COM

GENRE BENDER?

JOIN VLES.COM

TOTALLY ENORMOUS EXTINCT DINOSAURS

December 2012

13 TH LIVE AT WEBSTER HALL
New York

14 TH DJ SET WITH CLAUDE VON STROKE AT THE MID
Chicago

15 TH LIVE AT THE SHELTER
Detroit

19 TH LIVE AT THE FONDA THEATRE
Los Angeles

20 TH DAY ZERO FESTIVAL PLAYA DEL CARMEN
Mexico

totallyenormousextinctdinosaurs.com

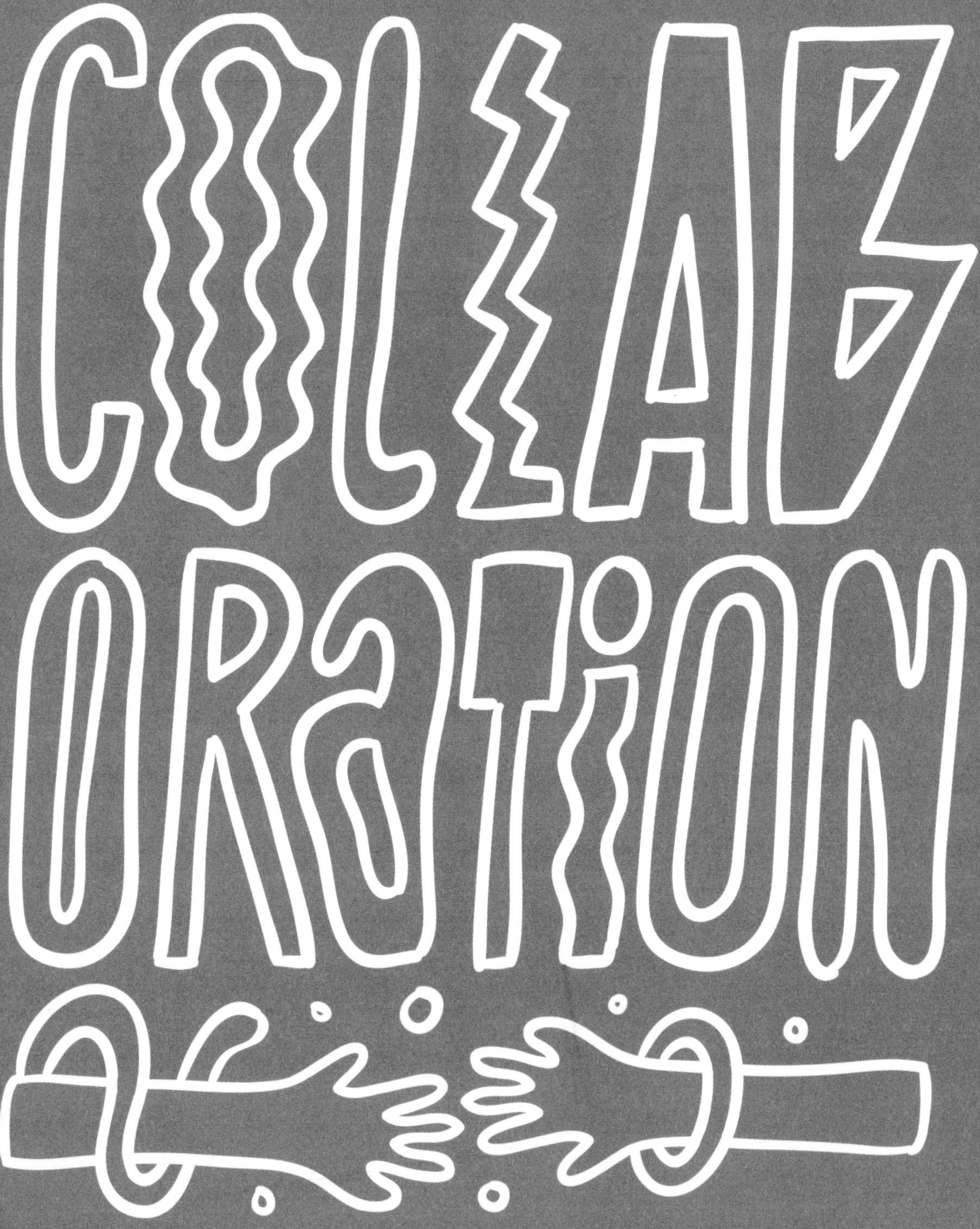
COLLAB
ORATION

No matter what field you go into, learning how to work with people is a crucial part of becoming a creative practitioner. Adding another person to your team can expand your skill set, but be aware that working with people whose work is similar to yours can be tricky. Choosing someone with a different style altogether can often produce better and hugely rewarding results.

Chromatics flyer
(with Alex Sushon), 2008

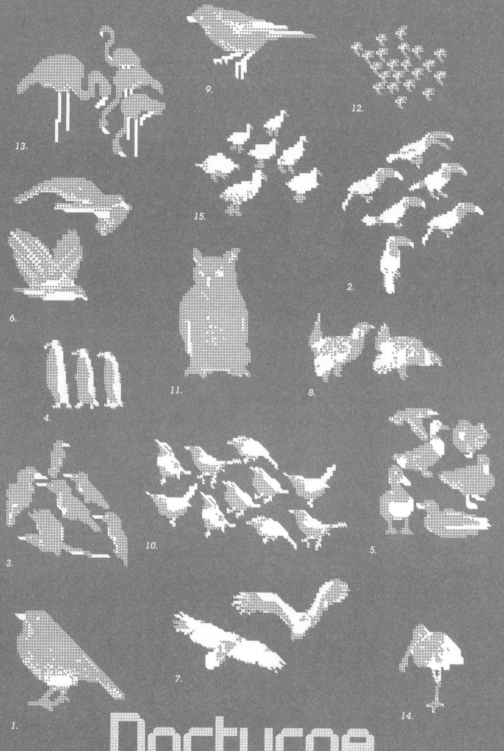

WHITECHAPEL COMPILATION

I met Alex Sushon, aka Bok Bok, who went on to found the record label Night Slugs, in 2004 on a summer course at Central Saint Martins. I had just finished my GCSEs and he was halfway through his AS levels. We hit it off straight away. At the end of the course I invited him and his friends to come and stencil a mural in my bedroom, which was brave of me, as I still lived at home and I hadn't really asked my folks if it was OK first. However, since I had spontaneously painted on the walls of my bedroom on a regular basis, I assumed it would be all right. Over the years, we've stayed in contact.

Alex was a big reason why I did my degree at Camberwell — he said it was OK and I admired him, so I applied. I got in and we have spent the last few years as excellent friends and collaborators. It's rare that I find people that I can work with whom I feel will commit as much as I do. That's the control-freak-cum-workaholic in me speaking.

Back to the point: the Whitechapel Gallery had been looking for someone to design the packaging for a new compilation CD they were putting out. They had actually pitched it to both of us without knowing we were friends. We decided that we should suggest a collaboration. It meant less money, as we would be splitting the budget in two, but a lighter workload, and it was exciting to be doing a joint project for a client. We were sent the music and listened to it independently, planning to meet the following day to discuss it. When we sat down together we both had exactly the same ideas — a perfect start!

The *Nocturne: Late Nights at the Whitechapel* compilation included music from a selection of artists who had played at the events. The artwork was designed following the bold Whitechapel branding. We deconstructed the gallery's logo, which was built from squares and triangles, and generated a series of birds using the 45° and 90° geometries. Each bird was designed based on the character of one of the musicians. The artwork was printed with two-spot Pantones, which we were very happy about.

Opposite: Pull-out poster
from the compilation CD
(with Alex Sushon), 2007

SMD VINYL

Simian Mobile Disco approached me to create an image that would represent the title of their album *Temporary Pleasure*. We sat at the studios The Premises, coming up with some really bad ideas — until someone suggested a giant bubble. I knew that bubbles are tricky to photograph (and bursting bubbles are even harder), so I called up photographer Jane Stockdale to take the pictures. She had done so much research we knew we were in good hands.

Sometimes you will have an idea that you don't think you can realize on your own, and this is when you need to collaborate with other people to make it work. I am an OK photographer but I am not a professional. These days, I would rather hire people to take great pictures than hire myself to take mediocre ones.

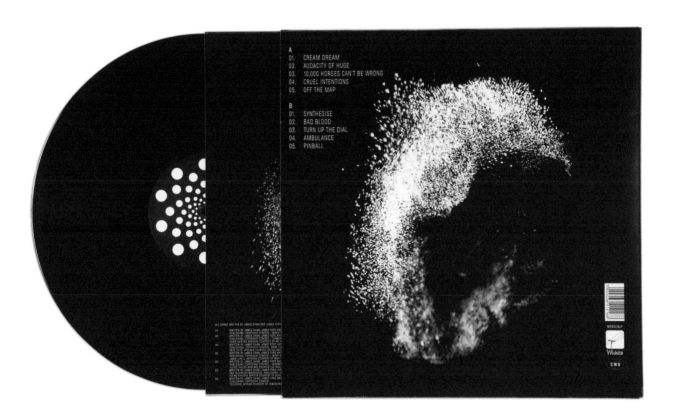

ADIDAS BALTIC CUP

Adidas approached a few artists and designers to design shoes for its project for the London 2012 Olympics, Adidas Consortium. I was assigned the Baltic Cup, a handball shoe that's slim and clean: a good canvas for print.

I set to work but quickly developed a theory that the first pair of trainers anyone designs will look like a rainbow. That's how it was for me; I exercised no restraint whatsoever.

After some early attempts, I was reined in by the Adidas team (I went crazy!) and produced this simpler, subtler design. Adidas were totally right to challenge my initial approach and in the end I was really happy with both the collaborative process and the resulting shoes. I even gave them an outing, running in them as an Olympic torchbearer.

KATE MOROSS X TOPSHOP

There are a couple of things in my career which popped up out of the blue, and I have no idea how the stars aligned to make them happen, because I had only wished for them in my wildest dreams. An email from Topshop while I was still at university was one of those things. I can remember exactly where I was when I got it (at my friend Milo's house having a cup of tea) — but of the message itself, all I can now recall is that it mentioned the words 'capsule collection', 'music' and 'illustration'.

Several meetings with the Topshop team resulted in seven unique designs applied to T-shirts, vests and jumpers for a Kate Moross x Topshop capsule collection.

I wanted simple silhouettes, nothing fussy or fancy: tees, jumpers and vests. I wanted boys to be able to wear at least two of the cuts and I saw a few taking them home, so that made me really happy. A lot of the process of designing clothes is about what is popular and what sells well, so I focused on the drawings and Topshop worried about the rest. All I wanted was to create items that were wearable, affordable, bright and intricate.

You can't expect your dreams to come true without putting in a lot of hard work first.

R.NEWBOLD
X KATE MOROSS

R.Newbold is the Japanese sub-label of iconic British designer Paul Smith. It was started after Paul Smith purchased a factory from Robert Brewster Newbold in 1991. The factory had specialized in developing military wear, overalls and other utilitarian garments. The label filtered out of Europe in the late 1990s but continued to flourish in Japan. Since then it has collaborated with other designers and brands to create small R.Newbold x collections, and in 2009 the team got in touch with a Kate Moross collection in mind.

I was asked to design a summer capsule collection and I worked very much in collaboration with the in-house team at Paul Smith to develop ideas for it. Unfortunately for me, only a few select pieces made it to manufacture. However, I was really excited to finally have created some quality cut and sew pieces — and also to have made some headway with good Japanese exposure.

SMD PHOTOS

I approached the year 2009 with a list of goals, one of which was
to work alongside a band as artistic director for a full album campaign.
That very same month, Simian Mobile Disco's manager called me and
asked me to be just that.

Jas and James of SMD are dream clients. They know what they want
and they also know what they don't want. Within those parameters, they
have flexibility and interesting ideas. They think beyond 'something that
looks cool' and really focus on the concept and semiotics of the artwork.
More than anything, they appreciate the importance of design and
understand its role in music.

NIKE DUNK BE TRUE

Don't wear Adidas shoes to a Nike launch party. More accurately, don't wear Nike shoes that look like Adidas shoes to a launch party.

Nike ideas man Acyde and I had been chatting regularly since we'd first met, and one day our coffee meeting and catch up trailed on a little longer than usual. I think my hair might have stood up on end when he told me that he had a project he'd like me to work on.

Now this was a serious project. Nike is nearly always among the first handful of clients name-dropped on the CV of someone that has had the opportunity to work for them. This is not just because of its global presence, but because it isn't the easiest client to sign off. Nike has high standards in every way and you must endeavour to meet them in everything you do when working for the brand. They expect the best.

Acyde had put together a dream team for this particular project, with Carri Munden (aka Cassette Playa) on styling and casting duties and Neil Bedford (Billionaire Boys Club, BAPE) as the photographer. Each person in the series was interviewed and photographed. It was my job to take Neil's photos and the interview transcripts and translate them into 23 unique portraits in the style of a magazine cover. In other words, I had a LOT of work to do.

DUNK XXIII

MY STYLE is UNCONTROLLABLE I'VE BEEN A NIKE MAN FROM A LONG TIME AGO I WEAR DUNKS WHEN I'M JUST CHILLING OR RIDING MY BMX

JME

I'M AN ARTIST I THINK more ABOUT WHAT I'M SAYING THAN WHAT I'M WEARING BE TRUE

I'M A MUSICIAN I DO MUSIC AND I'M STILL OUT IN THE MAIN OFFICE

DUNK XXIII

I GET FRESH WITH COLOUR

I DON'T JUST KEEP THEM IN A BOX

I THINK TRAINERS ARE NICE TO LOOK AT I DRESS FOR MYSELF

THESE I WANNA WEAR A PAIR AND BRUISE AND WAS THAT AFTER

NEW JET

DUNK XXIII

I AM AN ARTIST I IMAGINE WITH HALF

KESH

COLOUR DIDN'T EXIST till we ARRIVED

I'M A MULTI SKILLED TOOL LIKE A SWISS ARMY KNIFE

IF YOU LOOK DIFFERENT IT DOESN'T MATTER WHAT YOU WEAR BE TRUE

WE MET IN 2003

ZEZI

I GUESS WE ARE JUST COLOURFUL PERSONALITIES

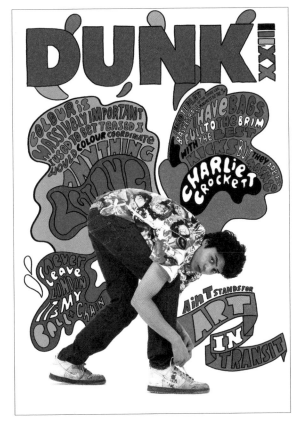

DUNK XXIII

COLOUR IS MASSIVELY IMPORTANT I USED TO GET TEASED I WOULD COLOUR COORDINATE ANYTHING & EVERYTHING

I USED TO PLAY BACK IN THE DAY... I HAVE BAGS FULL TO THE BRIM WITH THE BEST KICKS BUT THEY ALL GET WORN

CHARLIE CROCKETT

I NEVER LEAVE LONDON IT'S MY BALL + CHAIN

AIN'T STANDS FOR ART IN TRANSIT

I am learning all the time. Self-education should never end! This is a really important thing to embrace in your career, so don't be afraid to learn on the job. Just because you haven't done something before doesn't mean you can't learn to do it now. Challenges are what makes work rewarding; doing the same thing over and over again is NO FUN. I often get asked why and how I work in so many different media and the answer is that it's because I like the process of learning something new, and I understand the potential new aesthetics that it can bring. If I don't know how to do something but I know I could learn, when a client asks if I can do it, I say yes. This is how your work will reach new people. There is nothing wrong with being a Jack of all trades.

As you gain experience you may be asked to design additional outcomes for projects. Maybe your client needs a website, or perhaps they want you to design a T-shirt as well as a logo. Have no fear, the Internet is here. You can teach yourself just about anything with the help of online tutorials, message boards and forums. There is always a way to get things done, and don't be afraid of subcontracting (aka hiring someone else to do it). Collaborating with someone whose skills complement yours can add an entirely new dimension to a project (as the previous chapter hopefully demonstrates). You can't learn everything, but you sure can try.

Embrace the learning curve — you won't regret it. Making it up as you go along is a skill in itself.

Sometimes you don't have what you need, but you just have to MAKE IT WORK.

SILVER CROSS

This job came in 2008 while I was spending some time in New York working from my friend Daisy's apartment — which was cool, except that she didn't have a desk. When it came to drawing, this proved a problem that needed to be solved, so I went to the shonky furniture shop / dollar store next door on Second Avenue and bought her a dining table. This became part of my office for the rest of my stay, and it was on it that I penned this illustration for Silver Cross.

However, even with a nice desk to work on, I still had another obstacle to hurdle. I usually scanned my drawings to put them into Illustrator, and I didn't have my scanner in New York. This is when I first realized that on the road I could photograph my drawings and work them into clean black and white Photoshop files before putting them into Illustrator with Live Trace — an amazing discovery for travelling and drawing on the move.

SOUL
VOGUE
ACCAPELLA
BOUNCE
BEATS
30TH
CASSETTE TAPES
HARD
PROTO
GARAGE ROCK
BASS
CORE
PUNK
HOUSE PARTY
LINES
FRESH
VOGUE
MIX TAPE

VOGUE

In the few meetings I have had with *Vogue* and *Teen Vogue* in both the US and the UK, it became apparent that it was rare to find illustration commissions on its pages. Little did I know that they would have a project just for me in February 2010. The Brit Awards is as big as any music awards in the world, and *Vogue* is as big as any fashion magazine, so being asked to be involved with a project that combined the two was the best news I'd had in a long time.

Again, I was in NYC when this was commissioned, so I only had my laptop and a couple of pens with me. Keen to make it work, I cancelled some of my evening plans and made my hotel room an office. I drew all the illustrations on hotel letter paper, photographed them with a point-and-shoot and then cleaned up the pictures enough to Live Trace them. In the end I did several versions using a very steady hand and a mouse to clean up the type, rather than my usual Wacom tablet.

If you are vectorizing your drawings you can photograph your work instead of scanning it. This is much quicker. You may need to tweak the levels in Photoshop before you put it into Live Trace.

GAY AGAINST YOU POSTER →

I worked up quite a strange tour poster for Glaswegian music duo Gay Against You's 'Hetero Cola' tour. It deviates from my usual palette, as the band's Lachlan asked me to 'go Aztec'. The type nearly killed me and infuriatingly it changed a lot as I was actually doing it. Yup, that's not a typeface — every letter was individually (and painstakingly!) hand-drawn.

Be aware when drawing hand-rendered typographic posters that the copy may change. It may be worth using a draft typeface as a placeholder until the client can sign off the copy. This will save you a LOT of time redrawing letterforms in the event of last-minute text changes.

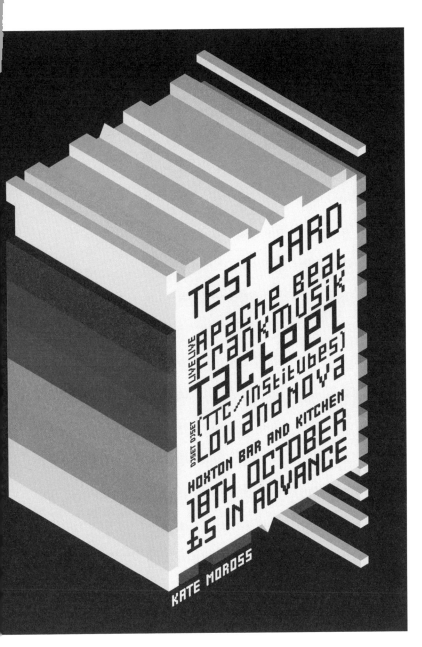

TEST CARD

For this flyer I thought I'd reference (and deface) the good ol' BBC test card. I had just discovered the 3D tool in Illustrator, can't you tell? This night was a one-off, so I only got to do one flyer, which was a shame. I wish I lived in a world that looked like this!

CONCRETE HERMIT T-SHIRT

For this, my first commercial T-shirt design, I had to buy a Pantone book.
I didn't even know what that was when I started the project! Perhaps
unsurprisingly to those that know me, my first interaction with a Pantone
book led me to use neon.

TRI HARD ERR →

Chris Knight of the gallery, shop and publisher Concrete Hermit was one of the first people I reached out to when I started illustrating, and he became a fast friend and supporter. After crafting me a button pack and selling the T-shirt featured opposite, he invited me to exhibit in his new shop / gallery in Shoreditch in 2008.

However, for the show I couldn't quite find it in me to draw on a canvas, the medium I'd intended to use. In fact, I really struggle with that format; it doesn't seem to work for me. Canvas is too bouncy and I end up feeling too precious about it, so I prefer drawing on walls or paper.

In the end, I created a mural at Concrete Hermit which was informed by a box of Brio Bricks for kids in the most amazing colours that I'd recently picked up at The Conran Shop. I put up a shelf and built myself a city using the toy bricks and then had explosive drawings bursting out from it on the wall. The building blocks also inspired a new T-shirt design.

As well as learning that canvas isn't a medium I feel comfortable working on, I also found out that cheap acrylic paints are not the best choice for murals. They can look streaky, although they do dry quickly and are easier than getting paint mixed. For murals I would recommend buying a thick, high-end acrylic such as those made by Golden, or choosing from a Dulux colour palette and having some tester tins made up for you instead.

T-shirt design inspired by my Concrete Hermit mural, 2008

Sometimes you may be asked to design something that has nothing to do with your everyday practice. As long as you can imagine it, you can probably design it.

LITTLE BIG PLANET

I was invited to build my own levels for the new PS3 game Little Big Planet. After attending a workshop to learn how to use an early prototype of the game, I spent days perfecting the mental mazes that made up the levels I was designing. I also got to design my own Sackboy character, who flew around on a rocket and burned in pits of fire.

BAPE DAISY LOWE

In 2011 the clothing label BAPE was launching a womenswear collection in the UK and its PR company was trying to put together the perfect team: Daisy Lowe as the model and face of the campaign, and myself and creative fashion team Silver Spoon sharing art direction and styling duties.

I had originally approached this project with the intention of illustrating all the pictures, so it felt natural for me to do the reference photography myself. It turned out that BAPE were so happy with the images I took that they wanted to keep the lookbook as pure photography. So unwittingly I added another string to my bow, and this photographic lookbook is now part of my growing catalogue of work.

VAUXHALL SKATE

Designing the logo for this event at Shoreditch's Village Underground was relatively straightforward, but painting the murals wasn't. We worked out of a garage in Angel in the cruel summer heat. Designer Jack Featherstone helped me to paint the car and the enormous wooden panels to decorate the entrance to the event.

The panels were so big that they couldn't be fastened together to be painted, as we would have needed a rig and a ladder to get around them. So we decided just to paint them randomly and hoped they would look good when they were put together. I'm not sure we achieved our goal.

Failure isn't time wasted. Whenever you fail to achieve goals, make sure you take the time to understand where you went wrong. That way, the next time you face similar challenges, hopefully you won't make the same mistakes.

GLASTONBURY

Designing a mural for a very large field at Glastonbury seemed daunting. The great thing about this project was that I didn't have to paint it myself, which was something of a relief. Luckily, the client employed a duo of awesome mural-painting specialists to hand-paint all my artwork from the digital files I supplied. When I showed up to the festival it was amazing to see it all done, and not to have to climb up a seven-foot fence to paint it.

PS: I don't always colour-coordinate my outfits to match my work, I promise!

Although it can feel weird to hand your artwork to someone else to render, specialists offer a service, rather like a printer. Learning to trust such people is important.

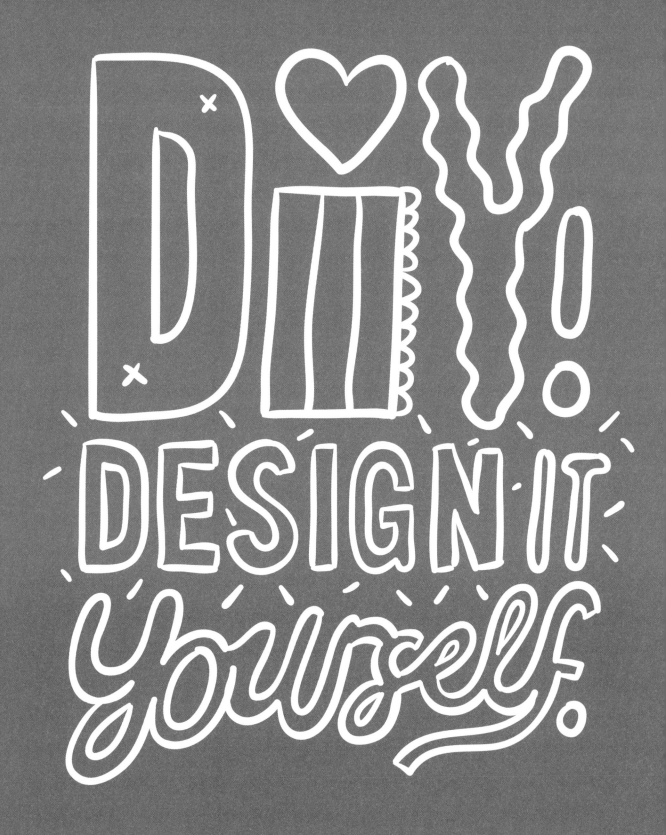

The DIY ethos is what brings all my work together. The idea of expressing yourself and creating work with the simplest means, and of learning how to achieve your own goals, continues to drive me. The notion that you have untapped potential to do whatever you want is a bit corny, but I've believed it ever since I was little. When I was perhaps nine or ten I used to have these trippy moments where I could feel overwhelming excitement that I was in control of my own future and could do whatever I wanted. I would sit and stare at my hands, and think, 'Cool, I can do anything.'

This confidence is very important: having confidence in yourself to try something and keep trying until you get it right, and not being afraid of getting it wrong over and over again. It is that determination that pushes you to finish a task to a high standard, to take risks and accept challenges. Whether it's a personal project or one for a client, you need to take these steps forward or you will not develop.

Learning how to do things is the key to your future. Let's be clear here: I don't mean formal education, but self-initiated learning. Building your personal library of skills and experiences will prepare you for your future as a creative.

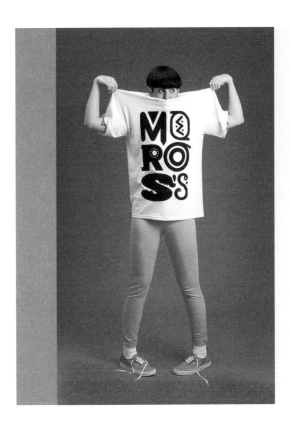

A photo from my DIY lookbook, for which I wore and designed the clothes myself

KM LOGO
AKA WHY TRIANGLES?

After years of not having a logo of my own, I figured it might be a good idea to design one. My love of this shape has been much scrutinized and debated. I have answered the question 'why triangles?' countless times, but I'm never sure what to say. It wasn't my intention to cause a resurgence in the use of the humble triangle, nor can I stake a claim to ownership of it as a graphic device. Ultimately it evolved from the isometric grid paper that I used back at secondary school to make isometric drawings.

During my second year at university, I did many experiments using isometric formations to explore Gestalt theory, which is why triangles started to make an appearance in my work. I was constantly playing with 2D representations of 3D shapes, both with type and abstract formations.

I was experimenting with a layered triangle as a device for a contents page on a potential book project. Out of that evolved a monochromatic layered triangle that has been said to be rather similar to the hazard symbol button you find on car dashboards. These choices were not conscious: the fact that triangles are used to represent 'danger' in common highway semiotics and diagrammatic language was merely a happy accident. I should also point out that I'm not a Freemason, nor a member of the Illuminati! Ultimately I chose the equilateral triangle because it is the simplest graphic building block. These polygons have been used by digital animators to develop objects and characters since the dawn of 3D technology. For me, the simplicity of this slanted shape represented what I was interested in as a graphic artist.

Original artwork by Kate Moross

SONY WALKMAN

I often use this project as an example of Design It Yourself. *Vice* was running an advertorial feature on the new Sony Walkman and had a basic brief and a spare MP3 player for me to play with. At its most simple, they wanted me to create something that represented 'happy'. Meanwhile, I knew that I wanted to combine photography and illustration, but as we didn't have the time or the money to have the product shot professionally, I had to have a think and see what I could come up with.

I had just upgraded to a new DSLR, a very useful tool if you are a designer, even if you don't moonlight as a photographer. This shot was as simple as me holding the player up with my right hand and photographing it with my left. I retouched the image, now that RAW image processing was made easy, and proceeded to draw all over it. Perhaps it looks amateur, but it didn't need to be anything else.

CUTTING PINK WITH KNIVES

These boys found me online — in 2005 I designed them a sort of filthy 'bump and grindcore' T-shirt — and now the band wanted me to design the record sleeve of their new album. After many caffeine-fuelled emails we settled on a small fee and booked in a day to shoot some photographs. Due to budgetary constraints, I was the photographer. On the day of the shoot, the boys turned up, and trailing behind them was Larry, their 'human mascot'. It was Larry that was to be the focus of the photo shoot. We put him in a tree, made him take his clothes off, the usual.

Please note that when I say 'photo shoot', I am not trying to insinuate that it was some grand event with lots of assistants and stylists. This photo shoot consisted of me, an amateur digital camera and a group of boys in a park somewhere in South London. At this young age, a 'photo shoot' was just that, but I still liked to use a fancy name for it.

The photos turned out great. The band had brought some origami birds with them, and we took these as a starting point for the graphics. I worked with the origami concept and created a booklet and a Japanese gatefold case. The booklet demonstrates the construction of the folds, and the back page can be torn off and used as patterned origami paper, but actually it's too thick, so I wouldn't bother. Had to put that one down to the learning curve!

You CAN do everything. As long as you aren't wasting the client's money or time, it's fine to try and do stuff yourself first. They will tell you if they want you to do it better.

Cutting Pink with Knives
Populuxxe 10" vinyl, 2007

I wanted to design record sleeves, so I started my own label in 2007. I called it Isomorphs because I'd seen and liked the word in the dictionary. I released five vinyl records over three years — until other people started recognising my work and hired me to design records for them. After that, I didn't need to have my own label, as I got to work with artists from all over the world.

HEARTSREVOLUTION, 'CYOA!'

I met Leyla and Ben of Heartsrevolution in New York in November 2007, shortly after releasing CPWK on Isomorphs, a new record label I'd just started. Coincidentally, months prior to our meeting, they had heard what I had been up to in the UK and had sent me a series of parcels filled with rainbow candy and stickers. The American in me is a sucker for care packages, but I had never replied, as they hadn't included a return address.

On meeting them I realized that they were the very same Heartsrevolution that had sent me the packages. That evening I apologized for my lack of thanks, and was invited into a world of neon lights and candy-coloured swirls. The duo had a release on the table with LA-based label IHEARTCOMIX that was in need of some artwork. I got involved.

HEARTSREVOLUTION, 'SWITCHBLADE', 10" VINYL →

My love affair with Heartsrevolution continued. After hearing their story about their delays in getting their record out in the UK, the words 'I'll release your record' fell out of my mouth.

The project called for some of the most expensive print I could afford. Leyla from the band and I worked together to build the concept for the sleeve. The holographic foil, called Gasoline Rainbow, depicts an open switchblade that wraps around the record. The Pantone 812 double strike on the inside glows as you pull out the record, like a cut in someone's skin.

Making specialist music packaging is
expensive. Find out the limitations of your
client before you start building the design
around some die cuts or hot foils, as most
of the time you will have to stick with
CMYK due to budget restrictions.

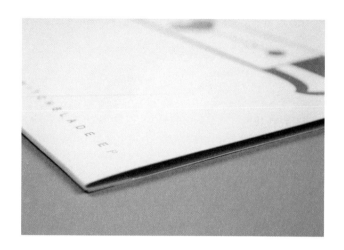

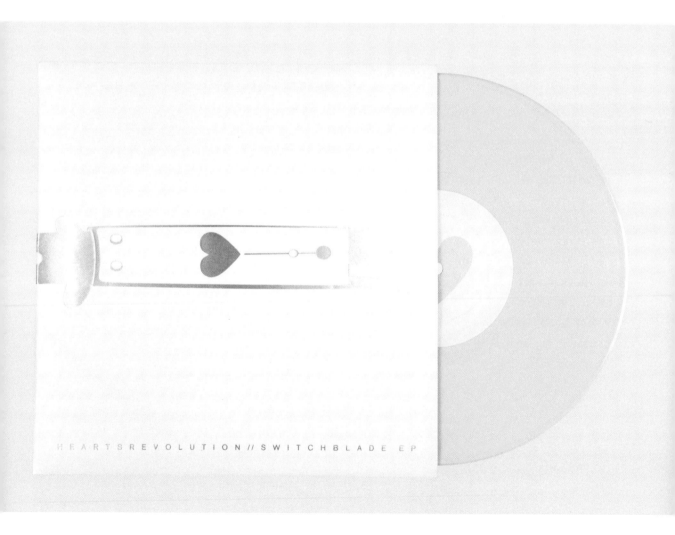

HEARTSREVOLUTION VISUALS

I think it's fair to say that Heartsrevolution enjoyed working with me, since they asked me to do some live visuals for their tour. I wasn't massively video literate at this stage: I could handle some simple stop-frame animation but that was about it. So all of the visuals for this tour were from photos and Flash animations. Something about them worked for the shows at the time, but looking at them now makes me shudder. These simple, stuttering videos were seen in large venues in Paris, SXSW in Texas and Koko in London.

Leyla and Ben were adamant that I be on stage with them for performances. To most people this would seem strange. Normally the VJ is relegated to the side or the DJ booth. Most of the time the VJ is simply a DVD set to repeat. I thought about this closely — I mean, I am not out on some 'I want to be a rock star' trip, and I was dubious about being on stage. After all, I am a designer, not a musician. After hours of turning the question over in my head, I realized that if we wanted the audience to know that the visuals behind us were live, I should be there in front of them, conducting from my computer and video console for all to see.

TOPSHOP MURAL

Having designed the Kate Moross x Topshop capsule collection (see pages 70–71), the next thing we needed to do was make a song and dance about it. I had made some suggestions in a meeting about possible ways to promote the collection, and I might have mentioned that it would be cool to draw a live mural in the Oxford Street store, or maybe paint up some mannequins and generally put on a show. Topshop took my ideas on board and just days after the final samples of the collection arrived, I found myself preparing to create my first ever mural in a huge window looking onto the busiest pedestrian junction in the UK.

I'd never done a mural or any 'live drawing', but thankfully I have some great advisors in the industry and I dropped my friend Jon Burgerman a quick email. It went like this: 'Hey Jon — how are you doing? Just a quick question: what's the best pen for drawing on walls? Black outlines mostly? Any ideas would be super.' Lovely guy that he is, his response was: 'I use Posca pens on walls. First of all you need nice, flat, clean walls, but Poscas will draw on pretty much anything. Where are you drawing? Keep me posted with your exciting exploits.' See, people are generally amazing and can help you out if you ask nicely.

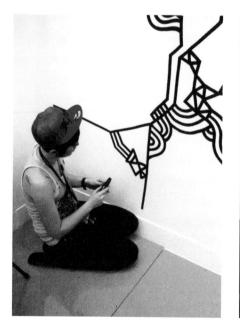 

The mural worked out great, even though I had no plan or experience. Sometimes you need to dive in head first, and don't be afraid to ask people for advice.

KM LOOKBOOK

OK, so I probably could have hired bona fide models to swan around in my clothes; perhaps a girl and a boy to represent the unisex nature of the pieces. But why do that when I am a boyish girl — and the clothes are my designs? I might as well wear them myself!

You don't necessarily need to hire a crew to make a lookbook. As long as you capture the clothing well, it can be simple to put together.

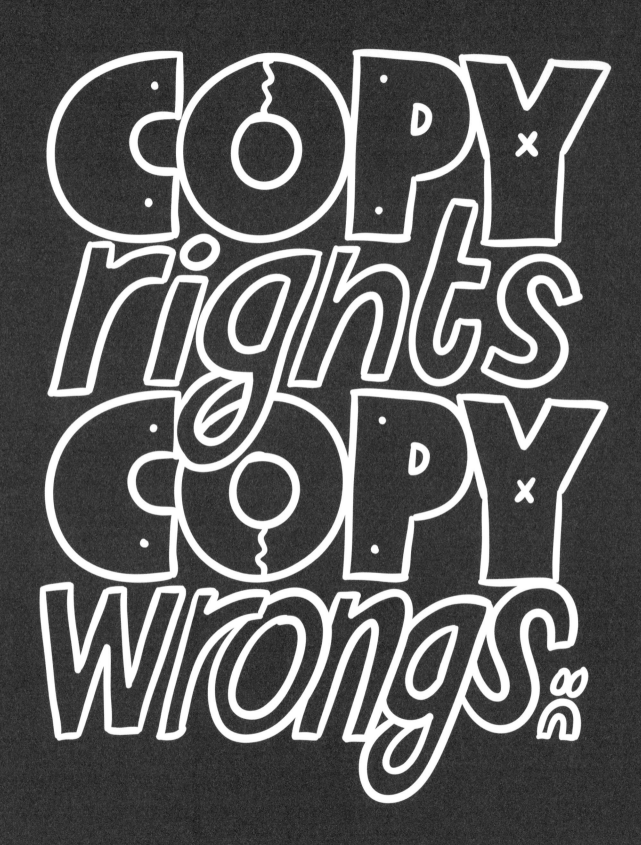

Welcome to the real world, folks, where nothing (it seems) is safe from copycats. If you create imagery and showcase it online, it is quite possible that it could end up being used without your approval, copied by another designer or even printed on a garment sold on the high street. Here is my advice on what to do when your work ends up being used for commercial gain by someone who thought you wouldn't notice.

Someone has printed my exact design on a T-shirt or other item that is for sale

If it is exactly the same design, unchanged apart from perhaps being stretched or squished (my personal favourite rip-off disguise technique), you have a few options. Firstly you can contact the seller or 'designer' of the garment with a fierce email saying that they are in breach of your copyright and that you suggest they remove the item from their store. In posh (legal) terms this is called a 'cease and desist'. You can write this in your own words, or you can use a template (just Google 'cease and desist copyright template').

In most cases, this will do the job nicely. Make sure to attach some image references of your original work. If you can, provide proof of when you designed it. If you have put images of it online, you can display the date that it was posted to a blog, for example, or your work might have metadata or a date stamp. Even better, if it was printed in a magazine, scan that, along with the cover, to prove the date it was published.

Most of the people who copy your work will be individuals who either made an error of judgement or who simply have no moral compass. Believe it or not, lots of T-shirt companies 'get' their designs by doing Google image searches.

Sometimes big corporations hire people for not enough money and expect them to come up with lots of ideas. This means that these people will copy and steal to meet deadlines. They think that because they work for a big company, they can hide behind the team of lawyers that it employs. The truth is that they can't. Any large company will be embarrassed that their employees are infringing the copyright of other people, so making light of that fact in the media is a good start. You have the power to get someone fired, or in serious trouble at their job, so do be aware of that before you start pointing fingers. You may end up feeling guilty. Then again, you may feel that justice is being done.

If you think you have a good case, contact a copyright lawyer and ask for some free advice. They will tell you if you have a chance, and a good lawyer will tell you honestly if their fee will be larger than the settlement. Be warned that lawyers cost lots of money, so if you decide to move forward down that route, be aware that just a few letters from your newly appointed lawyer to the infringer could cost you thousands of pounds.

If you don't have the money for a lawyer (who does?), and if communication with the infringing company or individual is going nowhere, another option is to kick up a big fuss on the Internet. Send your claim into www.youthoughtwewouldntnotice.com. Having a good rant might make you feel better. However, I'd only advise using this approach if repeated attempts at communicating in a civilized one-to-one way haven't yielded any results. Also, before you start slinging accusations of plagiarism, think carefully about what you're doing and saying. Unfounded accusations could land you in serious legal trouble yourself, so tread carefully!

If your case is strong, the brand or company will consider your claim and you may get a small payout. Do note that we aren't talking lots of money. If 700 T-shirts were printed with your design on them, say, you would only be entitled to a small percentage of the cost price of each shirt, so it's conceivable that a settlement payment could actually work out as being less than a lawyer will cost you. Try the cease and desist tactic first and see if the company will remove the items from their store and give you a settlement. Your settlement will usually include a gagging order, which means you cannot mention the case again. Make sure that you fulfil your part of the deal!

Having experienced both the lawyer and the personal route, I think that for most claims, contacting the company yourself is the best bet. Be headstrong and ballsy, show them that they are wrong for copying you and make it undeniable: send them all of your reference material and evidence, line up the artwork in Photoshop and show them that it was traced. The best possible outcome is that they will pay you some money, and will either continue to sell all the items until the production run is sold out, or remove the goods completely from sale.

Someone has printed something that is similar to my design on a T-shirt or other item that is for sale
If the design contains none of the original elements of your work, it is difficult to prove that it is copied. It may be useful to contact a copyright lawyer for advice on whether your case is worth pursuing.

Someone else's work looks like my work

This is different to copying and there's nothing you can do about it. You should probably take it as a compliment! Creating work and publishing it means that people can see it and be influenced by it. Being grumpy about it has the potential to make you come across as rather egotistical, so be careful how outwardly 'annoyed' you get. I actually collect copies of my work; I refer to them as 'fan art' rather than rip-offs. There are only so many ways to draw letters and figures and use colours. There will be work that is similar to yours, created both before and after your work, and that is just the way it is. If you want to make enemies, you can send mean emails to people who are imitating your style, but a better use of your time and energy would be to just keep on coming up with new ideas and new work. Plus, wouldn't it be embarrassing if they did it better than you? It happens!

If someone's portfolio is entirely filled with copies of your work, ask an unbiased person if they think that the work looks like a copy. If enough people agree, then it may be worth writing an email. In most cases, the person that is copying you will be a BIG fan, so be gentle. It would be sad to turn your biggest fan against you. It's most likely that they will take note of your comments and try to come up with some new styles of their own.

In the commercial illustration world, your work might be referenced in pitches for clients. On the rare occasion when they don't commission you to work on the resulting job, another freelance illustrator will be looking at your work in the pitch document and will be requested to use elements from it in their response to the brief. This happens: I have seen it at first hand. Sometimes I have turned a job down because the client wasn't right or I didn't have the time to do it, and a few months later I have seen elements of my influence in a design that someone else has done. Again, there's nothing you can do. Even worse, as a commercial illustrator, there will come a job where YOU are that guy, desperately trying to avoid copying the reference images in a brief, but being pushed towards them by the art director. This is all a very normal part of being a commercial illustrator.

KATE MOROSS SIGNATURE TEE

This design was originally sketched up by hand, but I decided to develop a new technique of tracing isometric shapes directly into Adobe Illustrator. Thanks to Illustrator, I was able to recreate them easily and they have been decorating my work ever since. I wanted to design a patterned T-shirt but with my name disguised within the design. Subliminal promotion can't hurt, right?

This was my first attempt to do so, and it works — some people don't even notice that they are walking around with my name inscribed on their torsos until a few weeks into owning the shirt! This first ever run was printed by Nascent Press in Dalston. I was certainly a rookie so far as sizing and placement were concerned; most of them sucked. I was also careful to keep my costs down, so I only printed S and XS sizes. 'Size-ist', I hear you say? Yes, OK, it's a fair cop, but I was keeping a wary eye on my finances. You will be glad to know that I now go up to XL and XS has been removed from my repertoire. Oversize y'all!

A quick tip here is to work your signature or logo into your T-shirt designs. T-shirt prints are the most commonly bootlegged work, in my experience. Your design may turn up on the high street or in a flea market in Thailand, you never know. I have nearly always designed my signature into the work, so if it is reprinted I can laugh at the lazy thief. With this project, I found someone selling the T-shirts as their own designs, and they had failed to realize that the main purpose of the design was to read Kate Moross … OOPS!

PUNKS JUMP UP T-SHIRT

This tee was designed in three-colour glory for the Punks Jump Up clothing label Stiff Couture in 2007. Using the release of the band's record on the Kitsuné label as a starting point, I took inspiration from the 12" sleeve and developed the design around it. Copied versions of this shirt have made the rounds in the UK, but also in places as far-flung as Malaysia. It has even been bootlegged in Korea!

TRIBAL PRINT

After using my isometric pattern work for a long time, I was keen to come up with a new motif: a pattern that could be applied to products and prints. The result was my tribal print; it is my most copied design.

DON'T PANIC POSTER AND ENVELOPE

Don't Panic became a regular client of mine. Their packs of flyers and event posters (handed out after club nights) kept me and many of my friends supplied with posters with which to decorate our bedroom walls at university. Luckily for me, in 2007 they asked me to work one up for them, so finally I would have one of my own posters to hang. The theme of the poster was 'War' and, always trying to avoid politics, I decided to lean towards 'Style Wars'. Having recently seen my work copied shamelessly in various posters around London, I figured this was a relevant take on the theme for me to explore. The poster took many hours of sitting on a bean bag in front of the TV slowly adding all the detail and colouring it in with the hundreds of Pantone markers I had collected over the years.

Think hard before referencing iconic graphic devices or silhouettes or the work of another designer or illustrator in your own work. You could find yourself in a spot of legal bother!

KATE MOROSS

125 MAGAZINE

This was a strange project in which I unwittingly ended up being the person in danger of infringing copyright designs. *125* magazine were commissioning portraits of artists, who were first shot in black and white by Cat Garcia and then illustrated by each artist. I can't even remember the title of the project, something like … Escape. I never really like these titles, because I worry that I'll do something naff. So I decided that if I could escape somewhere I would go to Disneyland. I drew pictures of Mickey and Minnie and gave myself mouse ears and a shiny nose. I submitted my entry to the magazine, only to find out that due to stringent Disney copyrights, they didn't want to risk printing it. So after lots of emails, I had to destroy my work, blurring all the pictures with the nudge tool in Photoshop so I looked like I was sleeping in some colourful sludge. Gone were the mouse ears and shiny nose, Goofy, Donald and Minnie.

Opposite: My original drawing, ears, nose and all

KATE MOROSS

Editorial work is hugely important in giving you exposure: magazines and newspapers reach very large and varied audiences. There are, however, drawbacks to taking on editorial commissions. The money usually isn't great, the deadlines are brutal and your work can easily get canned at the last minute. Cover commissions and large features are likely to bring in more cash than a small column doodle, but the size of the fee all depends on the publication. I personally LOVE editorial work, as most of the time the editor or art director that is commissioning you is asking you for your visual perspective on an article rather than dictating to you what they want you to draw. This is rare in commercial commissions, so it can make a nice contrast to drawing-by-numbers.

These are just some of the many editorial commissions I have worked on: everything from covers to smaller article illustrations.

New Year illustration
for *Wired* (with Jack
Featherstone), 2009

SUPER SUPER MAGAZINE

I don't necessarily recommend emailing magazines out of the blue and asking them if they fancy running a feature on you. Contacting *Super Super* magazine, though, was one of those occasions when I thought that it might be an all right tactic, and it paid off: the result was a three-hour chat over coffee in Soho with the magazine's art director, Steve Slocombe.

I wanted them to let me draw on a wall and take photos of me jumping up and down in front of it. They didn't go with my idea but instead ran a feature on me and my work, and I got to design a pull-out poster. Steve spoke to me at length about telling people what I liked, admired and referenced. Up to that point, I'd never made it easy for people to find that out; maybe that's why I encrypted my response into an isometric maze poster. At the time I had been reading about Abraham Maslow, and decided it was a good idea to make my own twist on his Hierarchy of Needs pyramid. I submitted this as my self-portrait instead of the comparatively stupid photo I had dreamed up earlier (see page 126). The issue suggested I was 'one of the hottest new design / illustration / art talents around'. I guess that's where I get my 'slash' reputation from.

Print media is one of the best places to get noticed by art buyers and clients. Contact editors, send them your work and take in your portfolio to show the art director; they could run a feature on you or, even better, commission you to create some editorial work. Just a note here: when you first start out, expect to be paid little or nothing for an editorial. As you progress through your career this fee will increase, but it will never be that big.

My Hierarchy of Needs
pyramid 'self-portrait'
for *Super Super*, 2007

THE HIERARCHY OF ARTISTS NEEDS AND THE PATH TO SELF ACTUALISATION

one must achieve all levels of the pyramid in order to progress onto the next layer. kate moross would also like to make a formal apology in advance to abraham maslow for abusing his theories for her own personal gain. the artist will take no responsibility for those who follow the path but never reach the orange bit.

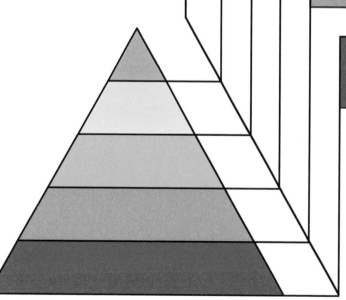

SELF ACTUALISATION
morals, creativity, spontaneity, problem solving, lack of prejudice, acceptance of facts, honesty, modesty, a good concentration span, pride, appreciation of science, economics, languages, physiology, sociology, a good pencil case, & a hot girlfriend.

ESTEEM
self esteem, confidence, achievement, brain space, some medals, a cup, a club membership, respect from others, your face in a magazine, 28000 plus profile views, your own mini fan club even if its just leesey, a dot com dot org or dot co dot uk.

LOVE/BELONGING
friends, family, (homo)sexual intimacy, hands, fingers, efficient tear ducts, free minutes, some jeffery brown comics, a heart shaped bed, silk sheets, and some mariah on the tape deck.

SAFETY
security of body, a job, resources, morals, a family (preferably a functional one), health, a roof over your head, a desk, a hot water bottle, one soft one hard pillow, a laptop and maybe a crackberry.

PHYSIOLOGICAL
gravity, breathing, food, water, sex, sleep, sugar, tea, homeostasis, shitting, pissing, smoking, and stationary.

VICE STUDENT GUIDE

The editor of *Vice* UK, Andy Capper, commissioned me to create
the cover for a student guide which also featured an interview with
me. You should have seen the first draft of the design — it was terrible!
Much as I hate being told to start again, my second attempt was far
better. The new cover was supposed to look like an old school textbook,
but it feels more tech / 1980s to me. The interview was conducted over
iChat — isn't the Internet a magical thing? I was also named employee
of the month by *Vice* on the inside of the cover — nice!

VOLUME MAGAZINE

Although print is supposedly dying, it seems that a new magazine pops up every second. Sometimes I'm approached for illustrations and, much more rarely, for covers. So when *Volume* asked me to do the cover of an early issue, I gladly took their offer. At the time I was working a lot with isometric hand-drawn shapes mixed in with situational hand-drawn type, and a new colour palette was emerging.

Vice Halloween 'Fear Issue'
cover, 2007

Next spread: Typographic
commission for *Wired*
feature on YouTube talent,
January 2013 issue

JAMAL
EDWARDS:
URBAN
MUSIC
MOGUL

LUKE
HOOD:
DUBSTEP
DIPLOMAT

TANYA
BURR:
MAKEUP
& STYLE
GURU

ALEX
DAY:
MUSICIAN

THEY ARE BRITAIN'S NEW SCREEN SUPERSTARS – A GENERATION THAT HAS BUILT A GLO

BY **TOM CHESHIRE**   PHOTOGRAPHY: **FINLAY MACKAY**   TYPOGRAPHY: **KATE MOR**

TOM
RIDGEWELL:
ANIMATOR
& SKETCH
WRITER

CARRIE
FLETCHER:
MUSICIAN

CHARLIE
MCDONNELL:
YOUTUBE
VLOGGER

LEX
CROUCHER:
MUSICIAN

...SE (AND A CHUNKY LIVING) ON THEIR YOUTUBE CHANNELS.

SO WHY WOULD THEY NEED OLD-STYLE TV STATIONS?

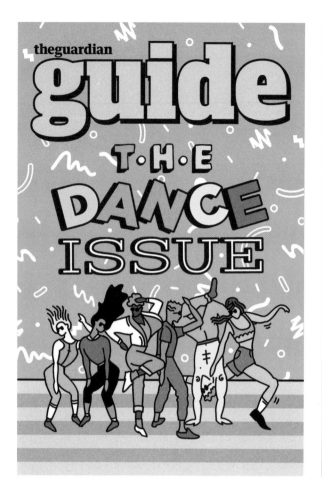

'The Dance Issue' *Guardian
Guide* cover, 2013

'1,000th Issue' *Guardian
Guide* cover, 2013

GUARDIAN GUIDE, AN A–Z
OF MODERN POP MUSIC →

Music is my work partner. Freelancing is a very lonely occupation and
music keeps me up, working and focused. Plus it's the whole reason
I got into this line of work. So when I was asked to illustrate this cover
for the *Guardian Guide*, I was stoked. It was a tribute to my early days
in illustration, but using my new methods.

theguardian

Saturday 30 June–
Friday 6 July 2012

guide

AN A–Z OF MODERN POP MUSIC

K-POP
POST-INTERNET#1
YOUTH SOUL
AFROBEATS
NIGHTBUS
ZOMBIE ROCK
MINIMAL WAVE
JUKE
DOOM
VOODOO HOUSE
EURO POP
INDIELECTUAL
the OOZE WAVE
CLOUD RAP
QUEER RAP
LAZER FUNK
UKBASS
TUMBLR WAVE
BROSTEP
GOTHGAZE
XENOMANIA
RETROLICIOUS
SKANDI PUNK
FUNKY
HIPSTER HOUSE

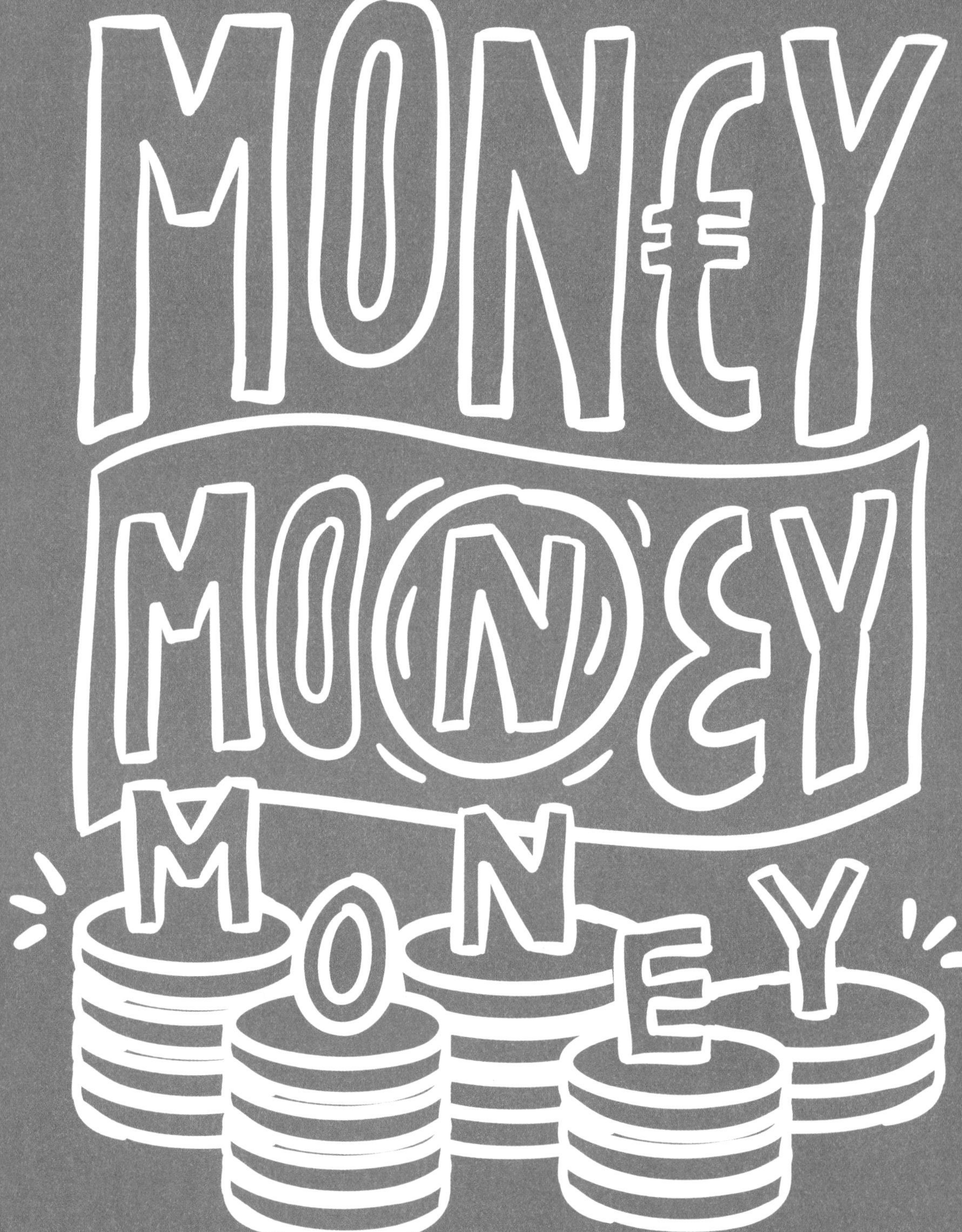
MONEY
MONEY
MONEY

FOR FREE OR NOT FOR FREE

It's a contentious subject in the creative world, but I have my own opinion on working for free. More than anything, this is a very personal choice, and everyone needs to consider their own policy on pro bono jobs.

My freelance career really took off during my second year at university, prior to which I primarily worked for free. I occasionally got a small fee, say £50—£100 for a flyer or poster, but at this time money wasn't an issue. I was still studying, so I wasn't yet worried about making a living while self-employed. I had the presence of mind to use this time to practice, developing my image-making skills and building up my portfolio.

Whether you work for free or not on a project is entirely up to you, but I would suggest that if you are working for free you should be doing it on your own terms, not on the client's. If you believe it is valuable work experience, then taking on an unpaid job can be worthwhile.

The other thing to note is that you don't even need a client — you can set your own briefs, make up your own projects and keep busy. When I was at college I would design logos for people without them even asking me to. I'd take photos of live bands and give them to clubs to use on their websites for free. I was doing everything I could and giving my work away to anyone who would publish it, simply to open up opportunities. When I bought my first Wacom tablet I used to draw pictures of people's social media profiles and post them on their walls. People started to think of me as an illustrator, and even though each sketch only took a few minutes to do, it had an impact. Gosh, I was such a nerd, wasn't I?

Looking back, it was my enthusiasm that people responded to. Many people for whom I created work for nothing early on ended up employing me for paid work later on. There was a return on nearly all of my invested effort. And there's another point to make, too: in a way, the jobs weren't done for free, because the opportunity to do work for someone or something interesting or fun was worthwhile in and of itself.

This whole process was instinctive: nobody told me how it worked or revealed a formula, I simply had the compulsion to make work, and I still do. And my confidence in myself and my work brought me naturally to a point where I could start charging people for it. Here is a selection of projects for which I received no fee.

UNDEREDUCATED FLYERS

This was my first foray into using isometric grids to create type. I had been experimenting in my sketchbooks and had spent hours staring at a Seripop poster that was on a friend's wall, and I wanted to have a go at something similar myself. I hand-drew the type, designing it letter by letter following the isometric grid I had built.

I ended up doing a couple of flyers for Undereducated. I did it out of love, because they let me do what I wanted and because I loved working in black and white.

If you are creating work you like, and you don't feel you are being taken advantage of, work for free. Even to this day I work for free. Ask for a trade, maybe some vinyl, maybe some tickets to some shows, maybe being on a guest list, whatever the client can offer you. And remember: if you're just starting out, the sooner you start working for free, the sooner you can start charging.

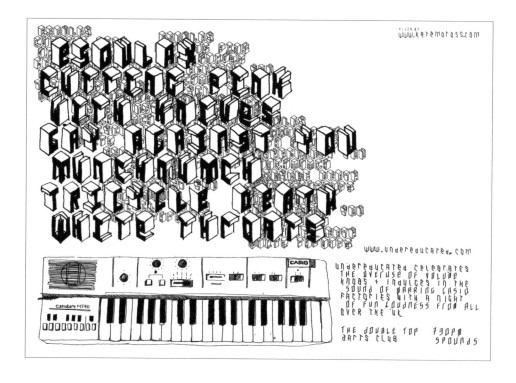

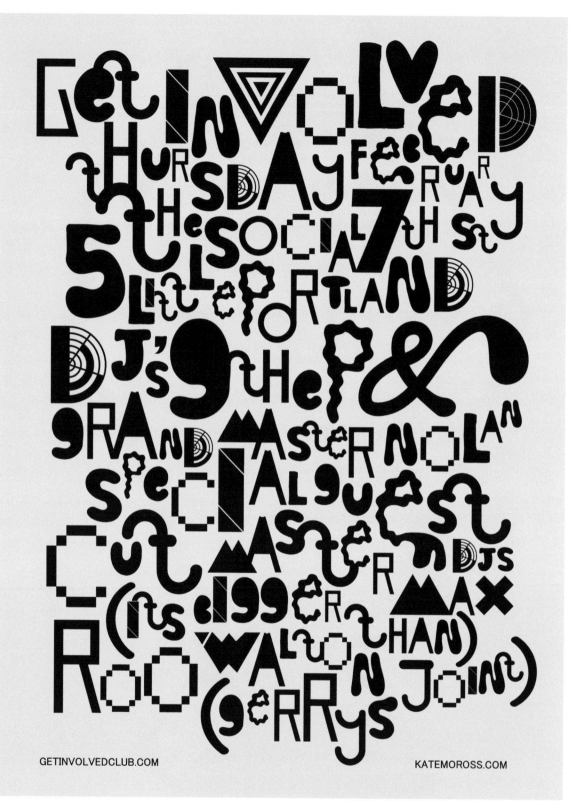

GETINVOLVEDCLUB.COM

KATEMOROSS.COM

GET INVOLVED

Gavin Lucas from *Creative Review* emailed me back in 2007 asking to feature the Cutting Pink with Knives sleeve (see pages 100–01) in a music-themed edition of the monthly magazine. We stayed in touch and *CR* picked me as one of its Creative Futures later that year, to be featured in the January 2008 issue.

As well as working at *CR*, Gavin ran a regular club night called Get Involved, for which he commissioned a different artist or designer to create each poster. I went on to design this poster, which featured a recycled mish-mash of type from other projects. It's almost a typographic *Where's Wally*: you could probably find each character lurking in a piece of my previous work.

Recycling is GREAT. I recycle unused work all the time — it really comes in handy for pitches or side projects like posters or pro bono commissions. Oh, and be nice to journalists and they will be nice to you.

NEW HERO MURAL ⟶

After letting me sleep (very well) on his sofa after Heartsrevolution played in Brighton early in 2008, I owed Ben from the band a huge favour. As winter set in, he called to cash in the IOU. A new nightclub in Brighton was opening its doors to the public, and he wanted a live mural painted for the opening of his night Strong Look. This was my first opportunity to get to know the Krink marker I had been saving for months. Designed for outdoor use and generally weatherproof, it was the perfect tool. In contrast to my chisel-tipped Posca markers, the Krink pen has a flat, round sponge applicator. It prompted a very different style, which is always a good thing.

Skills trading is a really
important part of being a
creative person. Generosity
can go a long way.

Elly Jackson of La Roux in
front of my New Hero mural

EASTPAK

I'm not sure whose idea it was at Eastpak to send out black canvas bags to artists for them to illustrate, as anyone who was at school in the '90s / '00s will know that the only thing that will make a mark on such a bag is Tipp-Ex. Yup, drawing on a black, water-resistant material is nearly impossible! Luckily my then assistant Max Gleeson took the bags home and dipped them in white emulsion a few times, meaning they were now all white, a little crunchy and porous but, crucially, easy to draw on. Good thinking, Max!

I decided not to do my usual patterns but to do something really simple instead, so I painted them in simple block colours with shading and highlights — which made them look really weird. They were put up for auction on eBay but I didn't like how little money they were going for after all that hard work, so I bought all but one of them myself! Someone else was battling me in a bidding war on the pink one, so after a few bids I let it go. It turned out I was bidding against my friend Lyndell. Well, it was for charity after all!

DITTO PRESS

My good friends Lynsey Atkin and Ben Freeman invested in a Risograph
printer and formed the now impressively established Ditto Press. Actually,
until they introduced me to Riso printing, I never knew it existed, but
I have since realized that it was the missing gap in my printing knowledge.
They wanted to do some press around their new company and had the
idea of sending artist prints out to potential clients to promote both
the contributing artists and their Riso printing services in one fell swoop.
In return for designing a print for them, I received a dozen to sell in my
shop: a perfect trade, if you ask me! This sort of deal comes along once
in a while, and I am all for it.

Swapping is awesome. I often
lend a design to a product
if I can receive some units in
return to sell in my online store.
Everyone's a winner.

I did it for nothing, and I made nothing, but thousands of people interacted with my work.

GRANIMATOR APP

I collaborated with UsTwo to make an artist 'pack' for its Granimator iPad app. While I was discussing the agreement with them, they suggested two routes: make it free or make people pay for it. It was my choice, and I decided to go for the free option, though it took me many hours to put all the digital components together for the app builders to create my pack. I wanted to share it with as many people as possible. My pack ended up being really popular, and for me that was more important than making a few bob.

RATES & CONTRACTS

Many people ask me for advice about what they should charge as a freelancer. Even to this day, in any facet of my work, there is no flat fee for a job, because design is a complex process with many variables. There are dozens of things to be considered before a final price is agreed. I hope that by using some examples I can demonstrate the best way to approach pricing from whatever level you are practising at. There are two ways to approach any job: day rate and flat rate.

Day rate

Your day rate is usually dependent on your experience level. A junior designer will be on a lower day rate than a senior designer. This is also the case for film editors, animators and many other freelance professions. There are also tiers in between. As your workload and skill level increase, you can increase your rates to match the scale of the project and your responsibilities within it. You will need to research your particular profession in more detail to determine your starting rate, and learn about the tiers and levels you can work up to.

Flat rate

Not all tasks will allow for a daily rate of pay. Some projects require a flat fee, which is agreed before the job commences. This is a more complex process in which you will need to make projections in order to create an accurate quote.

To quote for a fixed-rate job you must take into account your fees, materials and overheads for the length of time you anticipate working on it. This alone is a skill which you will get better at with time. Using a spreadsheet can help calculate all of these individual costs per day to find a final sum.

Contracts

No one wants to talk about contracts, but you will grow to realize that they are very important. Whether it is a written agreement sent in an email or a professionally prepared legal document, contracts are crucial in every industry. You need to decide which method suits your practice. Don't learn about this the hard way: make sure you have every agreed cost and project outcome of a job in writing. This can all be done via email — there is no need to actually send letters in the post.

If you want to take it up a notch, you can develop a terms and conditions document; templates for these can be found online and adapted. They are written in plain English, no legal jargon, and can be used to outline the costs, kill fee, deadlines and deliverables. Both parties agree on the terms and sign them, and they will provide clear guidelines should you and your client fall out at some point while you're working together. Be aware that you need to keep to your side of the agreement too — no slacking!

With flat-rate work I feel most comfortable when I invoice for a job 50% in advance. This is easier to achieve if you sign a terms and conditions document, since the client will then feel safe knowing you will uphold your side of the agreement. Then I ask for 50% on completion of the job before delivering high-resolution files. In my experience, most clients are happy with this process and understand meeting in the middle. Don't be afraid to ask for money upfront, especially on a long-term project. With fast-paced commissions you may need to waive the upfront fee in order to meet the deadline, since bank transfers can take a few days. You will have to decide which is the best route to take.

Some clients will not be able to sign third-party contracts; they may develop their own legal documents and ask you to sign them. Read them carefully and query anything you are unsure about. They may also not be able to pay you upfront. In these cases, you should request a purchase order (PO) number, which they raise on their side. This is a formal signal that they will pay you the amount agreed. Accepting a PO number is often an agreement on payment between yourself and the client.

If you have defined a kill fee, this protects you if a job is cancelled, or if you have creative differences. This kill fee could be the entire 50% deposit or a percentage of it, depending on the payment structure agreed and what stage of the project you are at.

Don't bore them with facts enthrall them with story.

IT Should BLOW YOUR MIND a little BIT.

Text illustrations
for Nokia, 2011

Converse Re-Imagine
artwork, 2012

CADBURY DAIRY MILK ⟶

I was still an undergraduate at Camberwell when I received an email which led to a commission by advertising agency Fallon UK for a nationwide print ad campaign for Dairy Milk. This is a nice excerpt from *Grafik* about this project:

'It's pretty big news for even the most established names in design to see their work on a nationwide billboard campaign, but when said billboard is proudly heralding its message outside the window of your second-year college tutorial, let's face it, you're in a pretty mindboggling place. It's a place that barely-in-her-third-year Camberwell student Kate Moross has inadvertently found herself inhabiting …'

I usually ask a prospective client to let me know their budget; then I tell them if it's too low or too high. You have to be very honest. At this time I didn't have an agent to handle these negotiations, so it was pretty scary speaking money with the big dogs, but I was upfront and confident.

Don't forget to register as self-employed and get an accountant. They can explain all the ins and outs of the financial side to you. Alternatively, you can file your tax return online yourself, which is quite straightforward.

Cadbury
DAIRY MILK
e250g
a GLASS and a HALF FULL PRODUCTION
eamy
Yummy

MAGIC TRIP POSTER

I love movie posters — somehow they remind me of my brother's 1980s
VHS collection — so I nearly jumped inside my computer when I was
asked to pitch for the *Magic Trip* poster. Independent films aren't exactly
big bucks, so it wasn't the money I was after here so much as the chance
to not only design a movie poster, but one for a psychedelic film about
Ken Kesey, the author of *One Flew Over the Cuckoo's Nest*.

WAR CHILD, 'ARMY OF YOU'

DJ and promotion duo Filthy Dukes joined forces with *Dazed & Confused* magazine to host a fabulous event to raise money for the charity War Child.

Charities are actually quite generous with budgets, more so than the average indie promoter. Just remember, they don't have to pay tax on it if you donate it straight back :D

So you want to be a freelance creative. This could entail being anything from a filmmaker to an illustrator, editor or type designer. Freelancing means being self-employed and hiring yourself out to work for different companies on particular assignments. Being self-employed is not to be taken lightly. It can be a very stressful and complex balancing act. In order to thrive, you must be motivated, confident, organized, skilled and great at communicating your ideas.

The ISO studio I shared, 2009

STU STU STUDIO

When I moved back to London in late 2007, I realized that I couldn't work from home — it was killing me. So I moved into a teeny little studio near Warren Street, big enough for two people, two goldfish and all my crap. Below my studio was an S&M dungeon and next door to me was a very elderly gentleman who loved nothing more than to wax lyrical about the 1960s and how they were relevant to my work. He even gave me an awesome book on the history of Carnaby Street.

After inhabiting my studio as a lonely hermit for a while, I started to invite more and more people to visit, share the space and hang out. It started to get a little cramped. There are only so many people you can fit in a 200-square-foot space. Working alone was no longer enjoyable and bouncing my ideas off people was really exciting and gave me even more of a reason to get out of bed in the morning. So I recruited two brilliant creatives, Jack Featherstone and Hans Lo, and invited them to share a new space with me, aiming to convince both of them that working in this environment was going to both improve the quality of their work and make them work harder. I succeeded in my quest. And so it was — we started working alongside each other and together as ISO.

Three years passed, and the studio had become a hive of activity, with new additions Max Parsons and Will Samuel. We were starting to move in different directions and outgrow the space. In 2013 we closed ISO Studios and went our separate ways. I went on to set up Studio Moross in our shiny office in Camden Town. With our small but powerful team of designers and organizers, we are creating some of our best work yet.

Opposite top:
My studio in my student
flat, 2006

Opposite bottom:
My studio in my student
flat, 2007

No matter how small or strangely located, having space to work is very important. Some people can work from home, but it's not my style. I like to keep work and home separate. I find the process of leaving the house and coming to work helps me to divide my life healthily.

hi!

My first proper studio
in west London, 2008

Top: The ISO studio
I shared, 2009

Bottom: Studio Moross,
2013

SAMSUNG OLYMPICS

In 2010 I was asked to pitch on the Samsung Olympic Visual Identity System, or SOVIS (since it's way too 'industry jargon' to keep on calling it by the full name). From what I could understand, Samsung wanted a Londoner or at least a Brit to come up with the SOVIS for 2012. What I misunderstood, however, was that this project was really meant for a studio rather than an individual, so the amount of work I had ahead of me was overwhelming.

After suggesting about four separate ideas, I was selected to take the project on. I must have come up with about 75 designs for individual logos and an overall motif. It was a beast and I wasn't succeeding: every time my rounds went off they came back with lists of changes. With every new design I had to show the work in context on a billboard, an advert, a brochure, a bus, a car, a flag — everything you could imagine! Multiply all those design rounds by every outcome and you have yourself a very large project indeed. After months of work, we started to narrow down the idea and reached a conclusion.

I was asked to present the final designs to the press at the announcement of Samsung's sponsorship of the Olympics. I dressed up in a shirt, bow tie and straw hat, my idea of smart. I arrived far too early and went to get a coffee. The lady behind the till asked me if I was going to a fancy dress party. Who goes to a fancy dress party at 7am? I wasn't off to a confident start. Then I had to stand on a podium and read off an autocue to the public and press. Justifying to the world a logo that was essentially an image of a mobile phone with arms is no easy task but I did it. And I did it all dressed like a clown.

Opposite: The SOVIS motif for supporting printed matter

This project was what I like to call 'a learner'. It was an honour
to be involved with the Olympics in my home town, especially
as I was nominated to be a torchbearer for taking part. Even
if the work wasn't what I hoped it could have been, I rose to
many challenges. Samsung is a massive corporation based in
a different time zone, with departments full of people who all
had input on the project despite a cultural and language barrier.
I managed to overcome most of those things to produce a piece
of work the client was happy with. That is, after all, the most
important thing.

FIRETRAP WATCH

When Firetrap asked me to design a watch, I couldn't turn the job down. Beyond screenprinting ready-made apparel or cutting some shapes out of plastic, I have always preferred to collaborate with existing brands rather than designing and manufacturing new products myself. That way, you get to realize things you could never afford to do on your own, because, let's face it, manufacturing your own products is very expensive. As a collector of timepieces I had wanted to design a watch for years, so for this job I ended up giving them not one design, but three.

Be aware when working with brands that they will put your name next to theirs on the product, so you need to be happy with the association. I always think that as long as you are happy with the product it doesn't matter too much about the brand who are behind it. If you can make something cool, that is why they are hiring you, so you can be cool for them.

THE BENEFITS
OF HAVING AN AGENT

When I started my career I was finding all the work myself, mostly through self-promotion or my friends and clients recommending me, and also because of a few positive (and flattering) press articles about me. When I did get an agent, the idea wasn't to get more work per se, but rather to manage all the work that was coming in.

As advertising jobs become bigger they get more complicated, with lots of formats and terms of contractual agreement that need to be fully understood and negotiated. A good agent will be able to deal with these complexities, increase your project fees and be a liaison between you and the client. If you can find a good one, an agent is a great asset to your practice. My agency, Breed London, has been amazing and I don't know what I would do without them.

I advise most people not to get caught up in the agency question, as either an agent wants to represent you and your work or they don't — it's hard to apply for representation. Work hard, pursue dream clients, promote yourself and make sure you have a good website and a PDF portfolio you can tailor to clients who want to see work in more detail. I got away with just my website for about three years but I also now have two physical portfolios that my agent sends to prospective clients all over the world.

If you do get approached by an agent, there are lots of elements that you need to get right. Here are five things to consider before signing on the dotted line.

Not too many, not too few

Some agencies have hundreds of artists signed up, some have just a handful. You don't have to think hard to work out the advantages and disadvantages of these two scenarios. Having lots of people on their books means they might spend less time specifically on you — but having a large roster might mean that they have many more job opportunities, even if you have to share them with 90 other people. An agency with a smaller roster of artists will allow more of a one-to-one relationship between you and your rep. They may not get the same volume of work through the door, but you will have fewer people to share it with.

What are the other artists like?

Make sure there's no one with work that looks overly similar to yours. This is very important. A conscientious agency will not sign lots of artists with similar styles or approaches, since they will end up competing for jobs. At the same time, be wary of an agency that hardly has any artists that do the kind of work you are capable of. If you are the only illustrator among graphic designers or photographers, for example, it may be that the agency has less experience in your particular field.

Where are they based?

Some offices are just based in one territory and this can affect the potential for foreign job opportunities. Some have offices all over the world. While this might seem impressive, be aware that this might not actually impact on the potential work influx, as different territories are looking for different things. Do look for someone that understands multiple markets with good connections in different territories, so you can get work from other continents — it's a big world out there!

Is it exclusive?

Will every single job that comes in have to go through your agent? Find this out straight away. You might have regular clients whom you want to continue working with on your terms, rather than your new agency's. It's possible to work out a deal whereby your agent only gets a cut of any work he or she brings to the table, while any work that you secure independently remains nothing to do with your agent whatsoever. Discuss all of these details and make sure you understand the terms of your agreement with your prospective agent / agency before you sign with them.

Last but not least, do you like the person you are talking to?

This person is your representative: they talk to your clients on your behalf and help you earn your living. You need to feel comfortable talking to them and believe that they understand you and your work and have your best interests at heart. The most important thing is to trust your gut reaction — if it feels wrong, it probably is.

YOU'RE FIRED

If you get into any disputes, try and find a neutral person to give you advice on how to settle any issues. Sometimes you have to make compromises in order not to burn bridges. This is all part of the job. Follow your instincts and make rational decisions.

In some cases a project will go down the wrong path. Maybe a client is just not getting your ideas, or pushing you in a direction you don't agree with creatively. I recall a client, after several rounds of rejected designs, asking me to draw a 'sexy girl robot'. I knew then and there that the project was over. You should try your hardest to meet the client's needs, but if, after multiple attempts, you feel that it isn't working, it is OK for you to walk away. In such a scenario you should be honest, direct and polite, explaining why you feel it isn't working. Clients will most likely be feeling the same as you, and stopping a project when it isn't working is much more efficient for all concerned than continuing down a dead end, wasting both time and money.

Avoid taking situations personally and learn from every process. Projects will fall through; you will lose pitches. Disappointment is a regular part of a freelancer's career. It is easy to over analyse rejection, but in most cases it is just circumstantial, so don't get too hung up on thinking of it as failure.

THE EGG HUNT

I have a couple of hangovers from my school days and one of them
is leaving jobs to the last minute. Not that I ever miss my deadlines —
but I do sometimes cut it quite fine.

This giant fibreglass egg arrived in my office and I had every intention
of painting it sooner rather than later but it sort of blended into the
background and I forgot about it. I remembered at the last minute that
I had two days until the deadline. So I furiously started planning it out.
It turns out that it's not easy to paint a square-ish pattern on a round-ish
egg and it took me a few coverups before I got it right! The finished egg
was displayed in Covent Garden Piazza and was seen by hundreds if not
thousands of passers-by. It sold well in the subsequent online auction
to raise money for Action for Children, too, and I went to meet the new
owner at the charity's headquarters to sign it and get a picture with him.
After a somewhat frantic start, it was a really rewarding project.

Sometimes when you are close to a
deadline, it is tempting to flake, or to
try and get an extension. I always prefer
just to have a late one, and try to pull
it off in time. I pride myself on never
missing deadlines. Order a pizza, turn
your speakers up and just get it finished.

BESTIVAL T-SHIRT

Lesson learned. Don't get complacent; check and check again. Especially when they are producing 5,000 units.

When I started out, designing a T-shirt that would actually be printed and sold was the Holy Grail of jobs. A few years later, the novelty had worn off, and picking out Pantone colours for each layer wasn't quite so exciting anymore. But by taking my eye off the prize, I actually made a mistake in this one; can you spot it? Luckily, we corrected the typo before it went to print.

Retro Super Future
sunglasses, 2012

DUMMY MAGAZINE ILLUSTRATION

'We'll need you to draw us something special — music related is ideal, but not necessary. If you have something else in mind, that's wonderful. After you've done that, we'll need to meet you for a chat about you and what you've drawn.'

This was all great. I did a drawing — not my usual style but still fun to colour in. As much as I insist on punctuality being a key part of success, I cannot always follow my own advice. I am normally pretty good at getting to meetings on time and meeting deadlines. However, occasionally someone will arrange an early morning meeting somewhere and it will either slip my mind or I'll just not wake up in the morning. This was one of those times. What a dummy.

Portfolio go-sees can be tiring, and I sometimes lose patience with them. This project goes to show that it is worth keeping going with them, because you might just land an amazing job.

KIEHL'S →

During my trips to New York and LA I make visits to agencies with my portfolio; this is an artist's equivalent to a model's 'go-see'. They vary from awkward flip-throughs to friend-finding. On my trip to NYC in 2008 I headed to the Kiehl's head office in Manhattan. My book seemed to go down well, and I had an inkling that they had a project in mind. I was familiar with Kiehl's from previous stays in the East Village, around the corner from the brand's flagship store. Sure enough, the in-house design team put forward a project which grew and developed as I was working with them, resulting in several projects, including this series of illustrations for all the flagship stores.

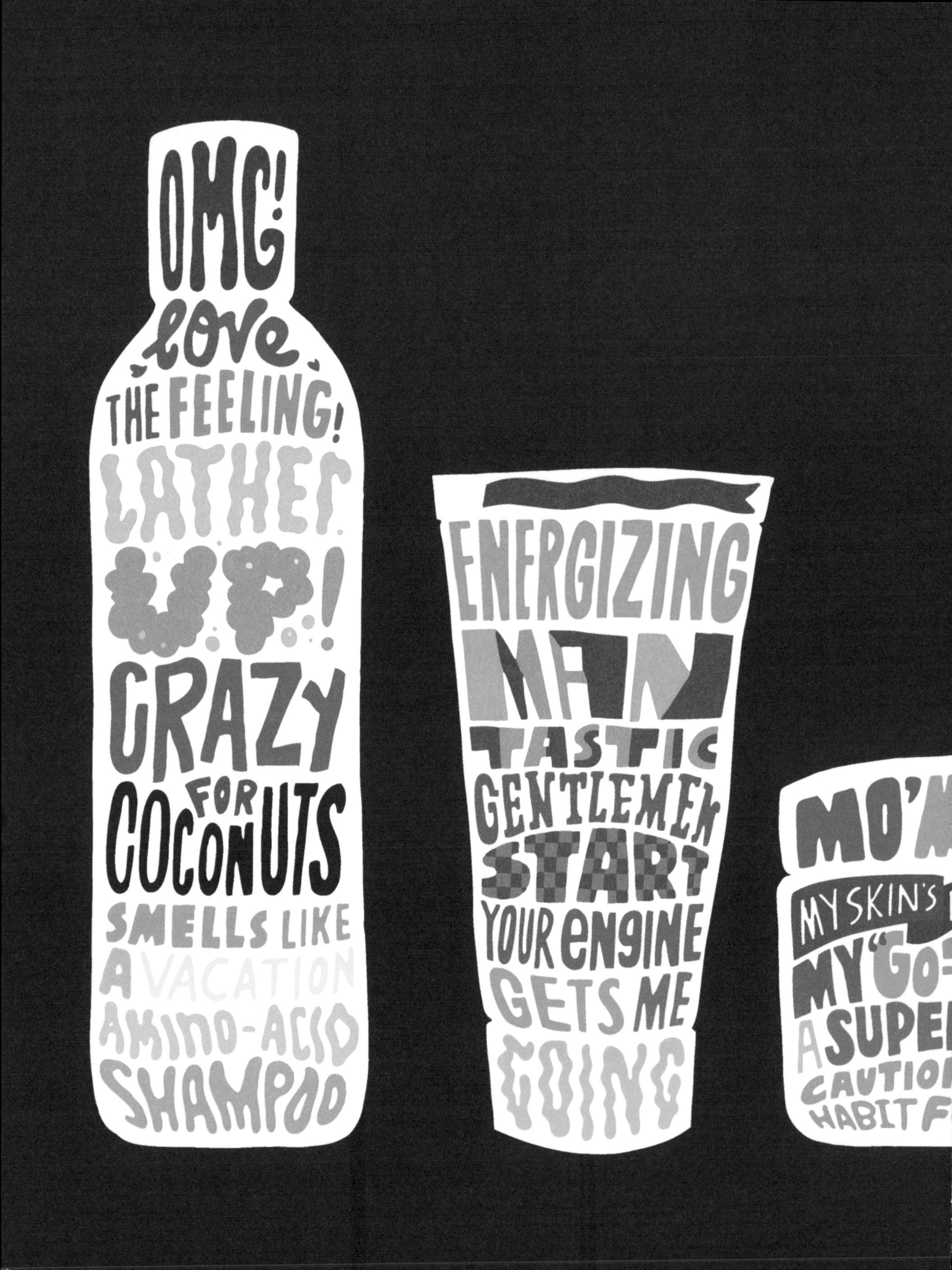
OMG!
love
THE FEELING!
LATHER UP!
CRAZY FOR COCONUTS
SMELLS LIKE A VACATION
AMINO-ACID SHAMPOO
ENERGIZING
MAN
TASTIC
GENTLEMEN START YOUR ENGINE
GETS ME GOING
MY SKIN'S

STURe
EAVEN!
CREAM
YDR8R
AY BE
MING
1C
THE
RESULTS
IT'S MY
SECRET
POWERFUL-STRENGTH
line reducing
CONCENTRATE
PACKED WITH
VITAMIN C
NO SIGN OF
FINE LINES
BYE BYE
WRINKLES
FAN
TASTIC
WORTH ITS
WEIGHT IN GOLD
MY BFF x
THIS IS THE
Cream of THE
CrOP
AMAZING
GOES A LONG WAY
EAULALA 4
Kiehl's
Since 1851

FREELANCING ISN'T FOR ME

For those of you who feel that freelancing isn't the path you want to take, that's great: the studios and businesses of the world need you! Gain experience and concentrate on team-based projects. Work across disciplines and get to know the job roles around you. Approach businesses for work experience and industry placements, and don't stop learning. A great CV and portfolio as well as the ability to work as part of a team is crucial if you're to gain a position as a full-time employee.

Popular studios usually have a long waiting list for paid internships, but don't let that put you off. Think of ways to stand out and tailor your portfolio and your communication to each studio. If you don't get a job in your dream studio immediately, don't worry. Designing full-time in most studios will provide you with valuable experience. Be persistent, but not too annoying. Email in advance to ask if you can drop off your portfolio in person, post a book of your work with a memorable message in a memorable medium, whatever it takes. If you get ignored, try again. If you get asked to leave them alone, then leave them alone! Step over the line and you risk leaving a negative impression, so look for the signs and respond accordingly.

Opposite: Text illustration
for Orcon, 2011

SELLING
STUFF
SALE
£

Once you have learned to design and draw digitally, how about making things in real life? It's easier than it's ever been to make the ideas in your head a reality. The Internet can connect you with low-cost manufacturers for anything you could wish for, whether it's screenprints, rubber stamps, button badges or a whole clothing collection — and you can organize the manufacturing from your desk. In the past these heavily industrialized processes required huge minimum orders at a high cost, but making smaller runs of a print or product is now within reach — and with the explosion in 3D printing, objects and prototypes can also be realized quickly and increasingly cheaply. The world is your oyster: you can make almost anything you can think of.

What I've found is that instead of making items from scratch, I like to collaborate with other artists or manufacturers to combine my design skills with their production skills and/or distribution networks. Making something is easy; finding a market for it, distributing it and actually generating profit is a whole different ball game.

KM triangle tee, 2007

143 PRESENTS

Before pop-up shops became the new cupcakes, I opened one with
my friends Damian and Avigail Collins, aka Silver Spoon Attire. A shop
in Ganton Street off Carnaby Street in central London was our home for
a few weeks in May 2009. We had a very small budget, so decorating the
place with lots of exciting shop fits wasn't on the cards. Instead I bought
five rolls of sticky-back vinyl, cut out hundreds of triangles and scattered
the walls and windows with them.

143 BIKE

I was sick of seeing unobtainable custom bikes that had been made for
brands and shop fits. I'm pretty sure that jealousy was fuelling that nausea,
because I hadn't been asked to design one and, let's face it, who doesn't
like designing dream bikes? So for the launch of 143, in partnership with
14 Bike Co., I fitted out one of their frames specially for the shop. With
a custom, hand-drawn saddle and some pastel-coloured accessories,
the bike was put up in a raffle. We sold tickets to raise money for charity
and at the end of the shop's term the bike was won by one lucky person.

MELON LEMON

Are you a melon or a lemon? This is a question we asked the public with two simple T-shirt designs created in collaboration with Avigail and Damian Collins from Silver Spoon Attire. I also designed them a new logo so we had something to print on the neck. Sometimes logos come out of nowhere.

We shot Daisy wearing the T-shirt right after the BAPE shoot (see pages 90—91). Combining jobs where possible can really help you save money.

TELEPATHE TEE

I designed this super colour tee for one of my favourite New York bands, Telepathe, to promote the EP release *Chrome's On It* on IAmSound.

Musicians often look to commission T-shirt designs from artists, since generic logo shirts are not very creative. The catch is that they usually don't have much cash to spend. Getting a small amount for a T-shirt design is OK, but I had an idea to make it more worth my while.

The T-shirt was only being released in the USA, so they weren't printing any shirts in the UK. I suggested giving them the design for free to use and print in the USA if I could print 50 T-shirts and sell them myself in the UK. That way I could triple my fee, as shirts have a great mark-up. Selling graphic design tees is hard, but when they have a band name on it's much easier. The band already have a following, and their fans don't care if the designer is famous or not; they just want to support the music.

HEART PRINT

I wanted to design a print to sell in the 143 shop, so as usual I opened up my triangle grid and got started Live Tracing in Illustrator. We screenprinted them in pairs and sold them dirt cheap, which explains why I don't have any left.

Making prints and posters of your work is worthwhile. You don't need to make everything large-format with lots of colours; keep it cheap. A3 prints with one-colour ink will be affordable to produce and ship. You don't have to make hundreds either — 30 will do — and the more limited the edition, the more special it will be to the 30 people that own one.

TRIANGLE NECKLACE

I worked plenty with acrylic at school, where we learned about the material's positive and negative properties and mostly made useless homeware. For my GCSEs I remember making some pretty serious Lucite furniture, line bending half-inch-thick plastic in order to craft bedside tables for my future home. My obsession continues to this day and I now realize that many of my interests stem from studying resistant materials at school. Since leaving school, acrylic has become my jewellery material of choice, with its multitude of bright colours and thicknesses.

A—Z of Heartsrevolution
T-shirt, 2010

SELLING PRINTS

Selling editions of your work is an excellent way to reach your audience and make a little bit of money. There are various different ways to approach creating prints, so here's a quick look at your options.

TYPES OF PRINTING

Screenprinting

Quite expensive to set up, screenprinting creates a really nice finished product with a handmade feel. A screenprint is created in layers of colour, each one printed separately. A silkscreen for each layer is made and printed in alignment with the previous one. Each screen you use will add to the setup cost, so the more colours that make up your print, the more expensive it will be to produce. It's best to design your work with the print process in mind. You can achieve better value for money by printing a one-colour design on coloured stock, perhaps with percentages of density, using what is called a half-tone. Because of the complex setup, screenprints are usually printed in an edition, all at the same time.

Giclée

Giclée is basically a posh term for a high-quality digital inkjet print. It's possible to create very high-quality fine art prints now from a digital source, whether it be a digital file created on your computer, a digital photograph or a scanned piece of work. They can be printed on a number of different papers and achieve a wide range of rich, deep colours. Giclée is fast becoming the standard format for fine art prints as they can also be created at archival quality. They are known to be the closest replication of the original source image.

The great thing about giclée prints is that they can be created on demand so as to reduce storage and upfront printing costs. However, they are quite expensive and must be handled with care in order to maintain their fine art quality. This is a great option for prints both large and small and can be offered with a framing option, as this will protect the prints and show them at their best. Giclée is a good choice if you want to sell in editions and at a higher price point. A giclée print can cost between £50 and £200 to make, depending on the size and quality of the paper used.

Opposite: New York giclée poster, 2011

Top left: Risograph poster,
1/100 limited edition, 2011

Bottom left: 'A—Z of
Video Games' lithographic
print for Shelter charity
auction, 2011

Right: Jessie Ware
eye chart screenprinted
poster (with Oliver
Chapman), 2011

Lithographic printing

This has a large setup fee, as a metal plate has to be created with your artwork on it. This is then inked and paper is pressed onto it to create the print. Really you need to print 500+ copies of something to make it cost-effective to print in this way, but after this number you will be paying very little per print: you can probably double the number you print for very little extra cost. Complex artwork can be reproduced accurately but it will not be as high-quality as a really good giclée. This method is most suited to posters or open editions that you feel will sell well over a long time period, or to a design you plan on sending out for free. I have had my monochrome tribal print reproduced in this way, and I sell it as a low-cost poster, even using it as wrapping paper for special gifts, as I have so many copies of it!

Risograph printing

A Risograph printer is a bit like a photocopier and a screenprinting machine rolled into one awesome device. The process is similar to screenprinting in that each colour is printed separately, so you can build up your image using separate colour layers. Each image layer is scanned through the copier on top of the machine and then a master is created by burning a negative image onto the master sheet. This master is then wrapped around a print drum of the desired colour. Blank paper is fed flat through the machine and the drum rotates, applying the ink to the paper, having squeezed it through the master. The colours are determined by the number of drums the printers own. They are quite specific and limited, though new colours can be created by half-tone and layer processes, and you can have your own custom colours made up in Riso ink drums too.

Risographs have become popular again since their more utilitarian use in the 1980s, and various new independent printers are now refurbishing old machines and setting up presses and small publishing companies to print comics, art books and prints. Most Riso printers only go up to A3, and the finished prints have a unique quality to them that is unlike any other print process. In a similar way to screenprints, it is their imperfections that make them so charming.

Risoprints are very cost-effective and can be great for gig posters, small books or comics. It is tricky to reproduce photographs using this process; they are better achieved in monotones rather than true colour. It is a great alternative print option if you want to keep your individual sale cost lower, and as the maximum size is A3, they're easier to store and cheaper to ship.

PRINT SELLING OPTIONS

Open editions

Any kind of print could be an open edition. All that means is that the number of copies isn't limited to a certain number — so you can sign them but you wouldn't number them. If you think it will be a print that you will become known for, you may not want to limit yourself to an edition.

Posters

This is my personal favourite way to print my work for sale. The difference between a poster and a print is simply that you print posters at a low cost, usually lithographically, in bulk, meaning you can sell hundreds of them cheaply, so more people can afford to own your work. In order to make a poster lithographically you'd have print a minimum of around 500 to make it cost-effective. It's unlikely that you'd sign posters as a matter of course — I prefer to sign on request.

Limited edition: giclée, screenprint, risograph

You select the number of the edition. If your work is in demand, a smaller edition can reach a higher price than a larger one. If you print all the work upfront, you can sign and number your prints in advance of selling them; if you print to order, you must keep a record and sign and number them as they are ordered.

Screenprinted bits
of recycled work, 2011

 Creating a commercial print is difficult, as you want to generate work that you are interested in *and* that the buying public will want to hang on their walls. I think we reached a happy medium with this piece and created an edition of 300.

OUTLINE EDITIONS

Outline Editions commissioned me to create a design for their 2011 London-themed exhibition. I was struggling not to create anything too clichéd but at the same time knew that something that was accessible would make for a better selling design. So I decided to make a detailed and colourful, if rather useless, version of Harry Beck's famous map of the London Underground.

Opposite: *American Psycho* design (screenprinted by Oliver Chapman) for Print Club's annual show Blisters — The Director's Cut, 2012

Top: CYOA! pixel T-shirt, 2008

Bottom: Isometric sweatshirt, 2012

Music has guided my career, from creating club flyers and designing record sleeves to art directing album and tour campaigns and directing music videos. Heck, I've even had a go at running my own record label, Isomorphs. If you had asked me as a teenager what I wanted to be when I grew up, I would probably have said singer first, designer second. After a few years of recording music in my brother's makeshift studio I realized I was much better at designing than singing, and I am thankful (you should be too) that I worked that out early on.

Of course, I am not alone in this drive to make music look good. This has been the path of many before me, some of whom have become design legends, proving that music is the perfect partner for the visual creative. It is a blank canvas with a brief. As a teenager I naturally gravitated towards the London indie scene — it was more than something to do and somewhere to go, it was a thriving community of enthusiastic young people with ideas, aspirations and dreams. Because music had been so important to me when I was growing up, I found this environment really exciting. The industry was tipping, small bands were making a big impact, club nights were packed and everyone was either in a band or a DJ or a promoter, or all of the above. Word gets around fast in a small community, and soon I was the go-to person for design work. I still work with people I met six years ago who have progressed in the music industry.

The more you immerse yourself in a culture, the more opportunities will arise, so get involved and become a part of it yourself. You never know who you might meet, what conversations you might have or what luck you'll make for yourself.

TINY STICKS VS MENTAL GROOVE

This was my first ever 12" record sleeve design, and though I have designed many sleeves, this is the only one that features my hand-lettered, albeit wobbly words. All the drawings were first illustrated with pen and ink, and then I discovered Live Trace paths and learned how to make my scans into vectors. This meant that my smaller drawings could be blown up big on a 12" cover without losing any detail.

ZOMBY SINGLE

There are quite a few bands that approach me to create artwork for them, but it is important for me to have a relationship with the artists, or a real love for the music, before I will work on a sleeve design. Partly this is so I don't oversaturate the market, but it's also because who I work for is just as important as what I create. Ramp Records slipped through my initial barrier purely because I was really into the MP3 that they sent me. At the time I had not heard of Zomby, nor did I know anything about the label, but something about both seemed really promising. Plus they were going to pitch me a bit of money on PayPal as a thank you. The result was one of the few collaborations I have done for the label and for Zomby.

JESSIE WARE, 'STRANGEST FEELING'

I rarely get to start from scratch creatively with an artist, so when PMR Records told me they had a new female artist that needed a direction, I jumped at the opportunity to get involved. Jessie had put out some pretty slick records with SBTRKT and Sampha, so was already on my radar. I started with a logo and, to be totally honest, this was no piece of cake. After six or more rounds we finally got there with the typeface Sackers Gothic. Sometimes you do pages and pages of creative and you end up choosing to use a simple typeface. That's logo design for you! However, on reflection I did misspell Jessie's name in the first two rounds, so perhaps I deserved it.

Jessie's label were keen to put out physical releases of her singles, so we had to make some vinyl packaging too, which of course I was delighted about. I met with Jessie to discuss her first solo single, 'Strangest Feeling'. After a jug of lemonade, we started to put something down on paper. Jessie had two ideas: purple and gold. I liked both of them. Knowing that true colour depth is best reached through photography rather than flat colour, I started photographing inks in petri dishes, mixing together deep blue and purples to make an indigo. The colours were so dark it was almost impossible to preview the prints, but the real texture was clear in the final product. I even painstakingly colour-matched the centre labels with the coloured vinyl and the sleeve photography.

Sometimes things don't happen instantly, but if you stick with them, it can pay off. Working with Jessie has been amazing and now I have designed her entire album campaign both here and in the US, directed several music videos and been a part of all her creative output. I could easily have flaked at the logo, but I kept at it.

HOOJ CHOONS

The Hooj Choons label was started in 1991 with lots of 'post acid house inspired enthusiasm and no money', according to their own website. They released over 130 singles and were massively important in European dance music before they shut down in 2003.

In 2006 they were preparing for a comeback and contacted me to design a new 'house bag'. At the time I was so new to designing for music that I didn't know what a house bag was. I assumed it was some sort of tote to carry records in. However I quickly worked out that what was required was a standard record sleeve for the label's 12" releases. Looking back at the artwork of the 1990s, my design inadvertently referenced the entire acid house genre without my knowing anything about it at the time. It seems to have been an amazing coincidence!

Within the label:

HACKMAN
iii. GUTTERFLOWER
iv. DUSK

b

© & ℗ 2010 PTN RAMP RECORDINGS
ALL RIGHTS RESERVED / PTN002

House bag for
PTN Records, 2010

SMD, UNPATTERNS

Studio Moross was asked to design three outcomes for collaborators Simian Mobile Disco's 2012 album *Unpatterns*. The music would be described as electronic dance, with leanings towards tech and house. The band create their music with loops and cycles using analogue synthesizers. The themes that run through their sound are pattern, repetition and distortion.

We wanted to create kinetic packaging that captured the themes in the music, so we created three animating outputs that use still images to create motion. The LP creates a moiré effect when the inserts are removed from the slip case. The CD can be rotated in the jewel case, also creating a moiré.

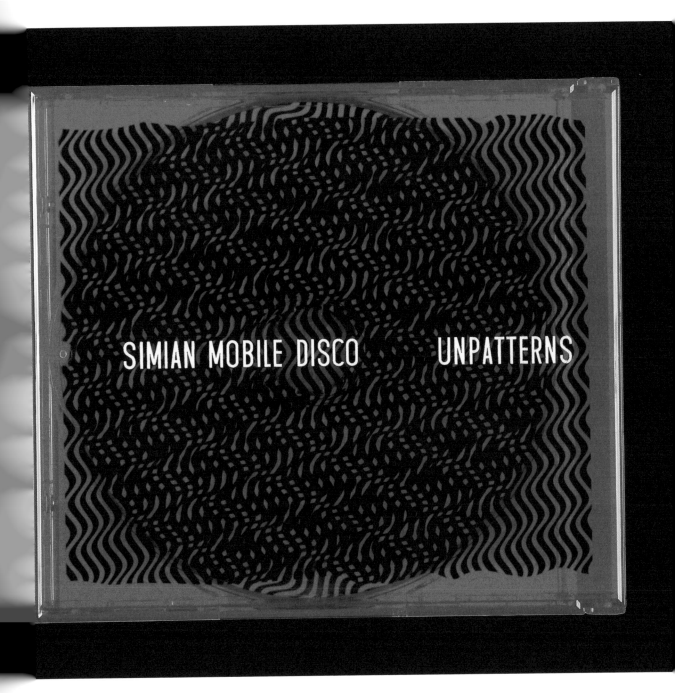

 Simple ideas can go a long way. Don't be afraid of a conceptual approach to a design problem. Aesthetics are not the be all and end all.

Risograph poster
for Tom Vek, 2011

MIDNIGHT JUGGERNAUTS, 'INTO THE GALAXY'

Heartsrevolution were supporting Midnight Juggernauts on the band's *Dystopia* album tour. The band was great. They liked what I had done with the *Switchblade* 10" sleeve (see pages 103—04) and wanted me to press a vinyl release for them.

For the resulting release, the band's single, 'Into the Galaxy', was carved into a black on black 7" with a pretty far-out remix from Architecture in Helsinki on the B-side.

These tiny, shiny, obsidian discs didn't sell terribly well, thus proving that not putting the band's name on a record in any legible form doesn't help sales. I still have lots left if anyone wants one!

PICTUREPLANE, TRUE RUIN

Musician Travis Egedy (aka Pictureplane) is, in my opinion, a god, so I was super excited to release his music, with all its weird warped 1990s energy. We chatted online about runes and symbols and strange occult imagery. I then created this sleeve for his EP on my label Isomorphs and, in an attempt to keep production costs down, printed it in black and white.

Top: Apes and Androids
7" vinyl, 2008

Bottom: Jessie Ware
12" vinyl (with Oliver
Chapman), 2012

making MUSIC VIDEOS

It is very difficult to make a career out of making music videos, as it is an incredibly competitive market, supported by the traditional film industry. Let there be no glamorous illusions about making music videos either. It is hard work for what usually amounts to very little money for such a large investment of time and creativity.

I myself have always been terrified of the idea of making music videos. This is probably because I've always understood that the moving image is, after all, a hugely challenging medium — there are so many parameters involved, from the narrative, photography, timing and edit through to actors, choreography, costume, soundtrack, sound effects … the list goes on and on. However, with the early videos I worked on, I was less afraid, as the films we were creating were labelled as 'experiments' from the outset. In time, I built the confidence in my filmmaking abilities necessary to develop bona fide music video concepts and bring them to fruition.

There are two ways of being a director. You can be freelance and produce your own films or use a freelance producer to put them together for you, or you can be signed to a production company. In the latter case every commission you receive will be produced by your company, who also represent you (rather like an agent represents an illustrator) and help you get work. On the next page are two examples of the music-video-making process.

There are several more routes, but these are the two most common.

MAKING A VIDEO
FOR A SIGNED BAND
IF YOU ARE WITH
A PRODUCTION COMPANY

The band or artist write a song that their label want to release as a single. The band will then explain their idea for the video (if they have one) to their manager, who will explain it to their product manager, who will then explain it to the video commissioner. The commissioner will create a brief, with some references to other music videos that they like and maybe a narrative or a theme that they want to include. The brief will also contain a budget, which will, more likely than not, be considerably less than you need to realize that particular video. The budget for an artist's video does not just depend on their popularity, but on how much they have left in their campaign money pot, if there's any brand sponsorship, how important the single is within the campaign etc. A music video budget can range from £1,500 to £150,000 and up, so it just depends on what is happening with the artist at that time.

The brief is then sent out to production companies or reps (who act as agents for their affiliated directors). They will be asked to get a specific director to pitch for the video, or sometimes the entire roster will compete, depending on the situation.

Then you generally have about 24 hours to come up with a pitch. This is typically several pages of writing and imagery, and links to reference videos for cinematography or edit style, for example. You will usually be sent a watermarked MP3 or stream of the song, which for me is the most important part of the process. Your idea needs to be exactly on point with what the band and label are looking for, which is very difficult, what with everyone in between distracting you. Then you will be assigned a producer by your production company, who will put together a budget and submit this with your PDF pitch. Some people even do video pitches in which they discuss their idea to camera, and include test imagery and sample clips with a fancy voiceover. I have done this twice — the first one I didn't win and the second one I did — but it was so exhausting I have gone back to written visual pitches instead.

If you are lucky enough to win the pitch, you will probably have to write it again after feedback from the commissioner, manager, band etc. Your producer will then rejig the budget accordingly (it will most likely be too high) and there will be loads of to-ing and fro-ing. The process isn't over until the contract is signed and the budget is approved. All this usually happens as the shoot date steadily approaches, and you will be frantically booking people to work on it in the hope that the shoot does indeed go ahead, worrying that if you don't do it in time you will have no one to actually shoot it.

If this sounds like something you would enjoy, then go for it. I have to say that it is a strangely addictive and enjoyable process, despite being a very complex and stressful puzzle. If you are lucky, the end product will be something you are proud of and it won't have been butchered by the 50 people who are constantly putting in their two cents. Watching the product of your labour on TV or racking up the views on YouTube is very rewarding, as is contributing to the sales of a record or the popularity of an artist. It really makes you feel like an important cog in the music industry machine.

MAKING A VIDEO FOR AN UNSIGNED BAND

The band will write a song that they and their management want to release. They will then work together with their team to choose a few directors to approach; they may even just pick one person. The band will work with the director to come up with a script or idea. As that director, you will have to then put together a short pitch document to illustrate the idea so it can be approved by everyone. You work to a budget, which is usually small, but within tight restraints some of the best ideas can emerge. In this scenario there will be no one in between you and the artist, except the producer (if you have one), which means that when they don't like something you will have to have the balls to negotiate changes and smooth out any disagreements. Hopefully in the end you will have crafted the concept that emerged in your treatment, and the video will function as a shareable promo for the band — and as a great addition to your showreel.

SMD, 'SYNTHESISE'

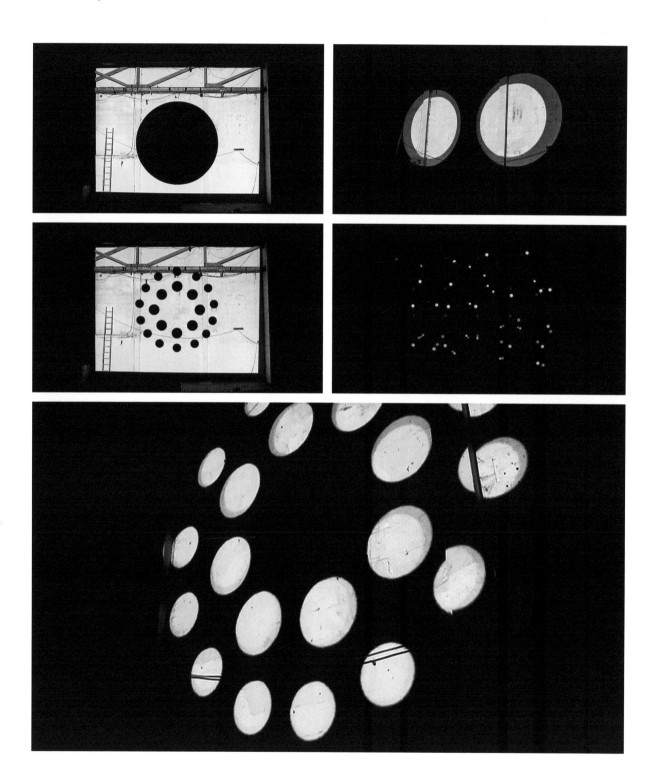

When Simian Mobile Disco approached me to make a music video for their track 'Synthesise', I jumped at the chance to work with them again, despite never having worked on a music video before. The concept for the album's artwork (for which I created the front cover image) was dots and circles, inspired by the duo's love of Yayoi Kusama. This was my first go at art direction, so I was making it up as I went along. I had this grand idea of a dot that travelled through space, bouncing around the walls and floors of a warehouse. I was nervous, as this was a big project to take on by myself, so I asked my friend Alex Sushon if he wanted to do it with me. He had proven a great collaborator in the past, so we agreed to turn our hands to moving images for this project.

We broke down the song into a detailed map of the stems (each individual layer) and designed simple animations that linked with each instrument. We then cut these up, no effects, nothing fancy, and layered them over each other for when each instrument played.

I animated most of the bouncy balls using Flash, and then Alex stretched and squished the video files in Ableton to match the track. It was simple and it looked right, so we kept going. Now we needed to find somewhere to film the projections.

Area 10 had hosted some very cold but very large parties in Peckham, South London. The warehouse had two massive rooms that were perfect for the shoot. We sat there in the freezing January cold in the middle of the night, filming the projections from multiple angles. After we'd edited the video, we knew it had been worth it!

Know your software, and fill the gaps in your knowledge when you need to. As a designer you need to have a good grasp of the obvious software packages and you should try and keep up to date. Lots of time spent working in Creative Suite and any moving image programs on different projects should be good practice.

Preparing a video can also raise lots of problems with size, format compression, etc. It might be helpful to try to collate all the specifications for all the different outcomes, and try saving your files and work to make sure you understand the various exports. It's not just the software you need to learn, but the output, delivery files and formats.

ALPINES, 'ICE AND ARROWS'

I can trace the path that led me to directing music videos back to when I was on the plane back from SXSW in Texas in 2008, where I had played some shows with Heartsrevolution as their tour VJ. On solo long-haul flights you always hope that you will end up sitting next to someone you want to chat to, rather than someone you don't, and on this occasion I was editing video files on my computer when the guy next to me leaned over and asked, 'Do you work in film?' It turned out he was Jamie Clarke, then of production company Pulse Films.

I think it was maybe a year or two later that Jamie was sitting in my studio asking me if I wanted to join Pulse as a director. He had kept an eye on what I was up to and had seen my Simian Mobile Disco films online, and was looking for new directors. Never one to shy away from new opportunities, I accepted the offer.

It's fair to say that I had no idea how the film industry worked. My experience until that date was messing around in some software I didn't really know how to use and watching over my colleague Hans's shoulder while he edited in the studio. Luckily my new career choice had coincided with the launch of affordable HD video technology, so I invested in a Canon 5D Mark II that has easily paid for itself since.

Having signed up as a director, I didn't actually get to make any videos for a while. Mostly I did a whole lot of talking, writing and pitching ideas. Pitching became second nature to me, but winning didn't. Directing videos is not, it seemed, something that you can get into quickly.

My first successful idea was for Alpines's 'Ice and Arrows'. I had trawled the band's blog for images and interests, learning about their music and aesthetic. They had provided a detailed brief, not to mention images of mountains, landscapes, ice, crystals forming, light and water. I was thinking that with the modest budget, producing this on a large scale might be tricky. Instead Hans and I researched shooting through a microscope, attaching the camera using a special adapter, and looked to create all these things on a microscopic level.

Mostly we just moved around some window cleaning solution and salt crystals in a petri dish and shot it all through a microscope in our studio, but it seemed to work really well with the track, and the band loved it too.

Music video stills
from SMD's 'Audacity
of Huge', 2009

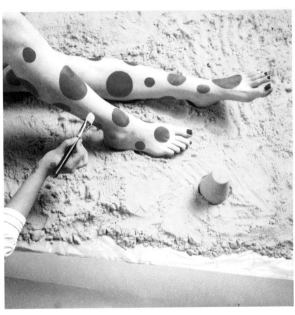

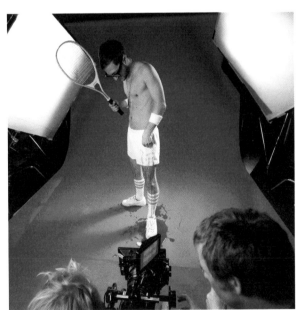

Behind-the-scenes photos
from SMD's 'Audacity
of Huge' music video shoot,
taken by Jane Stockdale;
although the video looks
polished, you can see how
silly it was to film in real life

JESSIE WARE, 'RUNNING'

Throughout your working career there will be 'first times' where you feel out of your comfort zone but will have to trust yourself. Ask advice and listen closely to those around you. It is important that you persevere through this; it is the best way to progress. Don't shy away from a challenge!

After our initial hiccup (remember how I spelled her name incorrectly?), working with Jessie has turned into one of my proudest success stories. When the label approached me with her initial ideas for the video for the track 'Running', I was split: Jessie already had a great idea for it, so it felt pointless to ask a bunch of directors to write pitches for what was already a clear and winning treatment. So I boldly put myself forward, suggesting that I could collate all of Jessie's ideas and find a great crew to realize them. Yes, I had only made a couple of experimental music videos, but I was yet to direct a 'real' promo with a proper crew, shot on location, involving an artist's performance. But that's exactly what I ended up doing for this — I even got a director's chair! Mostly I owe the success of this video to Jessie, as it was all her concept. I just sort of stuck everything together.

Music video stills from
Benzel (feat. Jessie Ware),
'If You Love Me', 2012

PICTURE CREDITS

All images © Kate Moross unless stated otherwise:

Image courtesy Adidas, © Adidas (pages 68, 69 middle and top)
© Guy Archard (pages 155, 159 top)
© Dave Brien (pages 94, 95)
© Eastpak (page 141)
© Cat Garcia (pages 11, 120, 121)
© Max Gleeson (pages 106, 107)
© Known (page 188 right)
© London Organising Committee of the Olympic and Paralympic Games (page 69 bottom)
© Margarita Louca (page 115)
© Magnolia Pictures (page 152)
© Media Molecule / SONY (page 89)
© Kate Moross & 14 Bike Co. (page 179)
© Kate Moross & Jo Apps (page 216)
© Kate Moross & Oliver Chapman (page 192)
© Kate Moross & Jack Featherstone (pages 92 bottom, 93, 123)
© Kate Moross & Ferry Gouw (pages 48–49)
Kate Moross and Hans Lo (dirs); produced by Pulse Films (page 215)
© Kate Moross & Marek Mysicka (pages 97, 108, 109)
© Kate Moross for Outline Editions (page 191)
© Kate Moross & Silver Spoon Attire (page 180)
© Kate Moross & Alex Sushon (pages 63, 65, 212)
© Kate Moross & UsTwo (page 143)
Jonas Mortensen (DoP); produced by Shimmy Ahmed (pages 218, 219)
David Procter (DoP); produced by Kate Moross & Jo Apps for ISO Films (pages 216, 217)
© Matt Ritson (pages 60 top, 101 bottom, 193 top)
© R.Newbold (page 72)
© Dani Rose (page 140)
© Laurence Stephens (pages 43, 67, 101 top, 102, 104 top and bottom, 127, 132, 152, 169, 197, 201, 202, 203, 205, 206, 207)
Laurence Stephens (DoP), produced by Studio Moross (pages 220, 221)
© Jane Stockdale (pages 66, 217)
© Topshop (page 70)
© Vogue (page 82)

THANK YOU TO ...

Mum, Dad, Daniel and Richard: you encouraged and supported me from the start. And of course to my enormous extended family, the Morosses, Lewisons and DeLanges.

Mable Cable — Colourful 4 Eva.

Hazel Falck, the greatest friend, advisor and supporter for this book since its conception several years ago.

Everyone who contributes so enthusiastically to helping me make great work, in particular Paul Gorman, Eike Konig, Alex Bec, Will Hudson, John Walters, Caius Pawson, Milo Cordell, Alex Sushon, Camilla Parsons, Chris Abitbol, Chris Hermit, Jessie Ware, PMR, Olivia Nunn, SMD, Oli Isaacs, Luke Williams, Scottee, Jamie Clark, Jenny Owen, Matt Fox, Matt Tillet, Skeet Skeet, and not forgetting good old ISO, Hans, Jack, Will and Max for New Cavendish times.

A big thank you to my friends new and old ...

Donna Rooney, Leyla Safai, Naomi Shimada, Avi & Damian, Daisy Lowe, James Connolly, Helen Ralli, Sophie Epstone, Harry Sprout, Dillard, Flax, Lizzie Capelin, Lucy Luscombe, Matt Taylor, Mahta, Margot, Camille, Tsouni, Heawood, and Tara Collumbell.

An extra special thank you must go to:

Ali Gitlow at Prestel for bringing this book together.
Gavin Lucas for helping me write the beast.
David Tanguy and Al Rodger at Praline for designing for a designer.
John Short for his work on the cover photography.
Oliver, Liv and Guy at Studio Moross for being the best team.
My amazing agent Olivia Triggs at Breed London.
Sabine Zetteler for the intro that brought this to reality.
Neville, I don't really know what to say! It's an honour.

Not forgetting the rest of my amazing friends, collaborators and colleagues.

© Prestel Verlag, Munich · London · New York, 2015
First published in 2014
© for the images see Picture Credits, page 222
© for the text by Kate Moross and Neville Brody, 2014

Prestel Verlag, Munich
A member of Verlagsgruppe Random House GmbH

Prestel Verlag
Neumarkter Strasse 28
81673 Munich
Tel. +49 (0)89 4136 0
Fax +49 (0)89 4136 2335
www.prestel.de

Prestel Publishing Ltd.
14–17 Wells Street
London W1T 3PD
Tel. +44 (0)20 7323 5004
Fax +44 (0)20 7323 0271
www.prestel.com

Prestel Publishing
900 Broadway, Suite 603
New York, NY 10003
Tel. +1 (212) 995 2720
Fax +1 (212) 995 2733
www.prestel.com

Library of Congress Control Number: 2013949327

British Library Cataloguing-in-Publication Data: a catalogue
record for this book is available from the British Library.

Deutsche Nationalbibliothek holds a record of this
publication in the Deutsche Nationalbibliografie; detailed
bibliographical data can be found under: http://dnb.d-nb.de

Prestel books are available worldwide. Please contact
your nearest bookseller or one of the above addresses
for information concerning your local distributor.

Editorial direction: Ali Gitlow
Text editor: Gavin Lucas
Editorial assistance: Lincoln Dexter
Copyediting: Martha Jay
Cover concept and art direction: Praline and Kate Moross
Design and layout: Praline
Cover photography: John Short
Production: Friederike Schirge
Origination: Reproline Mediateam, Munich
Printing and binding: Neografia, a.s.
Printed in Slovakia

ISBN 978-3-7913-4910-7

FSC
www.fsc.org
MIX
Paper from
responsible sources
FSC® C020353

Verlagsgruppe Random House FSC® N001967
The FSC®-certified paper Tauro has been supplied
by PapierUnion, Germany